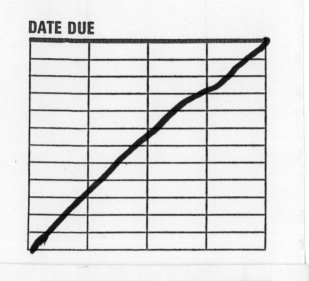

The Learning Center

A Sphere for Nontraditional Approaches to Education

The Learning Center

A Sphere for

Nontraditional Approaches to Education

by

Gary T. Peterson

Associate Dean of Instruction
The Learning Center
De Anza College, Cupertino, California

Linnet Books / *1975*

Library of Congress Cataloging in Publication Data

Peterson, Gary T.   1939-
   The learning center.

   Includes index.
      1. Instructional materials centers.   2. Audiovisual li-
brary   service.   3. Education—Experimental   methods.   4.
Curriculum planning.   I. Title.
LB3044.P47   371.3′078   75-22321
ISBN 0-208-01421-7

© 1975 by The Shoe String Press, Inc.
First published 1975 as a Linnet Book,
an imprint of The Shoe String Press, Inc.,
Hamden, Connecticut 06514

Printed in the United States of America

To my wife, Pat, who has always wanted the best for me

To Ollie Larson, who showed me how to be the best

To the Learning Center and Bob DeHart, who let both
of them happen

Contents

7

Preface

This is a book, or perhaps an essay, on a wonderful place —a learning center. In the book the writing will swoop from the conceptual to practical, from the general to the particular, from the center as it is to the center as it will be. The ideas should be of interest and help to those in, or planning, a center, whether that center be a gargantuan of fifty or more employees or a small one of but a few. Though the center is an idea, it is also an institution that exists. Based on the best which has gone before and dedicated to providing the best for its learners, it will succeed, making itself responsive to the individual users it serves.

The learning center is an amalgamation of four services: a library; audiovisual services; nontraditional learning activities; instructional development. Each in kind offers something important to an educational institution but together with a single purpose—to serve the learner in an individualized fashion —they are far more effective.

During the past few years the author has visited, written about, and at innumerable meetings discussed the center. But little of an organized fashion came from those experiences, and as De Anza College became a central focal point for those wishing to learn about the center, it became apparent that an organized discussion and appraisal of the center was needed. In January 1974, 450 people from all over the United States, Canada, and even England attended the De Anza Learning Center's Second Annual Symposium. That symposium finally crystallized for the author the need to put "it" down on paper. As the learning center is a cooperative effort, a sharing of needs and expertise, this book is a sharing of the conceptual ideas and the specific activities that have made the learning center succeed.

The Learning Center

A Sphere for Nontraditional Approaches to Education

Introduction

We are faced with a problem in education today which is a direct result of the verbal literacy movement. Mass communication (primarily television) based on highly articulate, bright and dazzling productions has developed new expectancies and literacies in its audience. Yet many members of that audience are in our schools today and are receiving their learning fare served up in lecture and printed page. To make education more palatable, to take advantage of the technology and system of the communications revolution, and to individualize as much as possible the delivery-response system, a new, more responsive administrative subunit of the schools has evolved: the LEARNING CENTER.

The learning center varies from a single carrel outfitted with learning materials to the large, multiservice organization now found in many community colleges; the name, "learning center," has many permutations such as the multimedia center, resource center, learning resource center, library, or audiovisual center. As an organized service it can be found from preschool centers to the university's graduate medical schools, from regional training consortiums to in-service centers for large corporations.

In most ways this book by considering the most comprehen-

13

sive centers covers most facets of any "lesser" type center. The logical extensions which can be drawn from the present volume should help anyone to develop the center needed to fit its learners' needs.

Earl McGrath, former U.S. Commissioner of Education concisely described the development of learning centers when speaking before a conference on learning centers (Gunselman, Marshall. *What Are We Learning About Learning Centers.* Eagle Media, 1971, pp. 3-5.) he said

The concept of the learning center involves several paradoxes. The most puzzling of these anomalies springs from the idea that institutions dedicated to higher education should find it necessary to establish an internal unit devoted to the very purpose for which the entire enterprise putatively exists. Are not colleges and universities established primarily to furnish the special facilities and conditions under which students with a wide variety of abilities and interests can make the maximum use of their time and energy in learning? The basic reasons for calling these relatively recent innovations "learning" centers are not entirely clear. One explanation must be the feeling among their advocates that these centers are especially effective in enabling students to gain something more in intellectual content and skills in the learning center than they would accomplish under conventional academic circumstances. Another explanation for the burgeoning of learning centers may be the growing influence of learning theory in highlighting the basic differences between teaching and learning.

Much teaching in college and university classrooms results in only a modest amount of meaningful, functional, and lasting learning. It is now demonstrable that even under the instruction of a teacher well-versed in his subject and dedicated to his job some students learn at a level of efficiency far below their potential. The reverse is also true; some students receiving instruction from teachers with less impressive formal qualifications and with quite unconventional procedures acquire an impressive body of knowledge,

master complicated intellectual skills and most important
of all develop such an interest in the things of the mind that
they continue to learn long after they have been weaned
from the classroom.

Another anomaly relates to the wide differences that
exist between the patently effective materials and procedures
employed in the relatively few existing learning centers
among the more than 2,500 institutions of higher education
and the materials and procedures in general use elsewhere.
The "culture lag" which the celebrated sociologist, William
Ogburn, identified in social institutions at large is particularly pronounced in the academic society. Methods of
teaching with the use of audio-visual aids, for example,
developed with millions of dollars of grants from the Ford
Foundation to mention only one investor, in spite of their
demonstrated effectiveness, have not been so widely adopted
as the evidence and investment would seem to demand.
(Benjamin S. Bloom. "Learning for Mastery," *Evaluation
Comment*, 1:2, May 1968)

But this is not in any way a revolutionary movement in education. Rather, it is a new administrative unit combining the
services and resources which have long been parts of the educational scene. To understand this, a brief, defining analysis of
this evolving center is presented here.

Historically, the movement has been a gradual, planned pro-
gression, beginning with libraries which placed emphasis on print
media, which reacted to requests and provided services for a
wide variety of consumers.

As the communication field enlarged, as we began to find
out something about the dynamics of learning, as technology
teamed with entertainment and sputnik-like hardware emerged
as ends in themselves, the educational community demanded and
received a wide variety of learning media. Combined with
libraries of print resources, this audiovisual boom with its con-
comitant stress on the individual teacher's development of new
software through local production resulted in the multimedia
library or center.

At about the same time a recognition that more nontraditional learning services and spaces were needed resulted in the rise of "learning resource centers." These centers were and are still dominated by media resources rather than service to the individual.

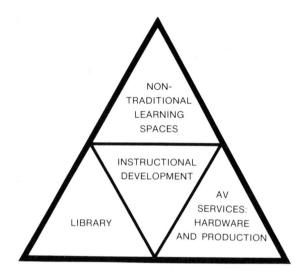

Figure I

Along with audiovisual product development such key ideas as programmed and individualized instruction produced greater developmental activity within the learning resource centers. With the stimulus of large infusions of federal money, the developmental activity became more systematic, and a movement in some organizations began away from the centralness of resources. In this newly emerging organization, the learning center, we see a strong combination of a library, an audiovisual program, nontraditional learning spaces and activities, and instructional development. This shift has been from *the* library to *the* learning center with *a* library of media. In such a center the emphasis is on *learning* as both a product and a process. Within the center with its consortium of specialists working toward the improvement of learning on campus, flexibility is a key asset of the organization. To understand this flexibility is to understand the concept of the learning center and its four major components.

1. *The library.* In a truly unified center, budgetary and media format boundaries should be eliminated. If money is available for commercial items, the most appropriate media should be purchased to meet the learning need. Thus, with one budget

THE LEARNING CENTER, DE ANZA COLLEGE

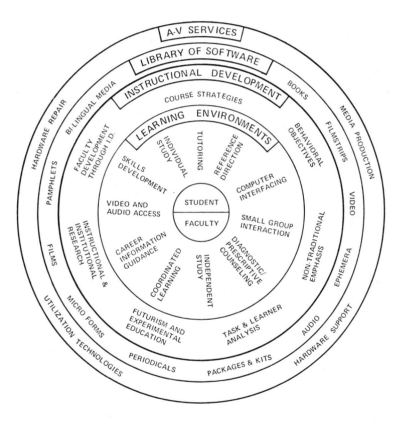

THE LEARNING CENTER IS A LEARNER CENTER

Figure II

for print and nonprint media, an audiotape capable of illustrating noise pollution might be purchased rather than a book or magazine which could only discuss the concept. As happens too often in many institutions, money will not be available for the tape, so an inferior item for that particular need will be purchased. Or if the business officer is not the culprit, tunnel vision which gazes upon but one kind of media may be the problem.

To extend this example then, the library of media can utilize the tape in some nontraditional learning space such as a learning or listening lab. Furthermore, if the tape were not available, it could be developed through the instructional development process and produced by the local production operation.

2. *The audiovisual program.* Within the learning center such a program is defined by its service status. It provides the major hardware support on campus and provides a production facility to supply the media of instruction and learning. Without the bother of promoting its own existence, it should be furnished the resources to provide electronic delivery of learning signals in a variety of learning milieus—from the large lecture hall to the individual learning carrel. Its production potential is enlarged to include printing, a press component (based on the idea of the small university press), microfilming, photography, multimedia packages, and computer program production, etc.

3. *Nontraditional learning spaces.* Though every learning center should have the four components discussed here, no area more that the nontraditional one exemplifies better the flexibility of the concept.

The learning center should be a center for innovation and experimentation. Thus, if one school so wishes, it may experiment with a tutorial center within its learning center. If the tutorial program is successful, it may continue. If not, it can be abandoned. Another school may wish to have a tutorial program and/or it may wish to institute a career center, an independent studies program, or a learning disabilities program. These programs become interdependent and strenghtened through interdependence. A linkage between tutorial services, educational handicapped services, and reading creates a totally more effective program. Thus, every learning center can be defined by the four elements, but no learning center would necessarily be a

DE ANZA COLLEGE LEARNING CENTER

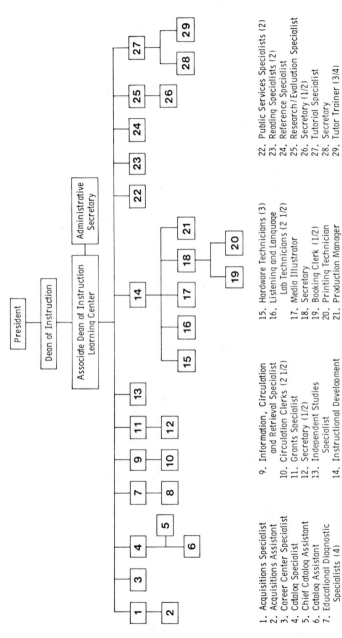

President

Dean of Instruction

Administrative Secretary

Associate Dean of Instruction
Learning Center

1. Acquisitions Specialist
2. Acquisitions Assistant
3. Career Center Specialist
4. Catalog Specialist
5. Chief Catalog Assistant
6. Catalog Assistant
7. Educational Diagnostic Specialists (4)
8. Secretary (1/2)
9. Information, Circulation and Retrieval Specialist
10. Circulation Clerks (2 1/2)
11. Grants Specialist
12. Secretary (1/2)
13. Independent Studies Specialist
14. Instructional Development Specialist
15. Hardware Technicians (3)
16. Listening and Language Lab Technicians (2 1/2)
17. Media Illustrator
18. Secretary
19. Booking Clerk (1/2)
20. Printing Technician
21. Production Manager
22. Public Services Specialists (2)
23. Reading Specialists (2)
24. Reference Specialist
25. Research/Evaluation Specialist
26. Secretary (1/2)
27. Tutorial Specialist
28. Secretary
29. Tutor Trainer (3/4)

Figure III

carbon copy of another one. And as long as this flexibility exists, the center should grow and evolve as a positive, success-oriented organization.

4. *Instructional development.* This area or service of the center provides for both the greater institution and for the center itself. Within the center it may help in developing media for the independent study program, for a library orientation class, for a skills program within the tutorial center, etc., and it draws upon the resources of the center for its system. Thus, the instructional development team may be made up of the center's research specialist, a print specialist, a nonprint specialist, a learning specialist from the learning disability program, a subject specialist from the teaching team, and the systems or instructional development specialist. With such a team, the learning system could be conceptualized, developed, produced, tested, evaluated, redeveloped, and reproduced.

As indicated here, specialization of functions is paramount to the successes of the center. As shown by De Anza College's staff chart, there is a great deal of initiative which must reside with the individual specialist. Yet these specialists should also have a broad-based generalist background so a commonality of experience can provide the ground for mutual trust, cooperation, and work.

This commonality of trust and singularity of purpose—the improvement of the learner's potential on campus—should carry across administrative lines. In the example the Learning Center is part of the instruction office, yet several of the programs which reside within the center are combined products of student personnel and instruction. The student is thus the winner and no one is a loser.

One of the common characteristics of specialists in a learning center is that they perform a number of administrative functions related to a variety of programs, and as quasi-administrators, they are not tied down by the precise schedule of the classroom instructor. If, then, the learning center has as a major role on campus the improvement of learning, it must act as a change agent. With a time schedule allowing for more planning and developmental activity and with faculties becoming older and more stable, an emerging function of the learning center should be in-service faculty development. The professional educator will be looking for new competencies, and the learning center should provide one system for such developmental activities. The future for learning centers is bright if their programs and personnel become heavily involved in the educational mainstream. But these specialists must be proactive more than reactive, flexible rather than rigid, visible rather than seclusionary, experimental and innovative rather than solid and unimaginative.

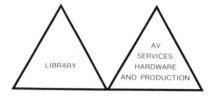

I

The Concepts

Library and Audiovisual Services

Purposes of the Learning Centers

The concept of the learning center has been analyzed as the four-part amalgamation of library, audiovisual, nontraditional, and instructional development services. But in reaching back even farther in explaining the rationale for such a center, six major purposes emerge.

1. The Learning Center provides *service* for faculty and students; this service supports the expressed needs of the LC's patrons and also provides resources which in themselves should expand the potentials and expectancies of patrons by suggesting new avenues for learning.

2. The Learning Center provides a variety of *individualized and individual experiences* for patrons through independent study, media resources, tutorial activity, etc.

3. The Learning Center through a variety of services supports the *instructional program* offered by academic areas. In special cases where course format, such as independent studies, or subject matter relating to the Learning Center itself, or for courses

which by their nature may be more easily offered via the low-cost channel of independent study, the center may itself offer courses.

4. The Learning Center provides leadership in the area of *media*, helping the faculty with evaluation, selection, and utilization of media appropriate to a variety of learning needs.

5. The Learning Center is concerned with *learning* as both a process and a product. The LC is particularly concerned with providing ways for students to become more effective learners in conventional classes, in independent study, and in the lifelong pursuit of learning.

6. The Learning Center is concerned with *change and experimentation* as vital forces on the campus. The Center collects and disseminates educational ideas from outside the school to personnel for their consideration and possible adoption.

Basic to such purposes are the print/nonprint resources and hardware and production systems which support those resources.

Hicks and Tillin laid out for us the dilemmic situation of libraries in a world where responsiveness to rapidly changing environments is necessary—yet change is so rapid that a reactive system will soon be far behind unless it develops a proactive posture.

Much has been said and much will continue to be said about the separate and combined world forces presently affecting libraries of every type. The impact of the computer has been described, the growth of knowledge and the flood of information statistically substantiated. Ideological and material changes have played their part, as have the possibly overwhelming demands that can be made on libraries by an ever-increasing population seeking new fields of employment, specialized skills, creative expression, and meaningful use of longer hours of leisure. The consequences to libraries of swelling enrollments in higher education and the extension downward of public education to three-year-olds have been estimated. Nor have the revolutionary ideas of youth lacked effect.

It is only natural that the library respond to these changes. Its very existence has always rested on the premise that it functions as a community agency reflecting the entire society

23

of which it is a part. To contribute to the total of man's life is the essence of library service, and this contribution can be accomplished by helping all people understand why revolutionary changes are occurring. The library practices this continuous guidance both by providing a record of man's cumulated knowledge and by ensuring that this record is communicated to each individual. (Hicks, Warren B. and Tillin, Alma M. Developing Multi-Media Libraries. R. R. Bowker Company, 1970. p. 3.)

But response to change is difficult. Some librarians have reacted negatively to the newer media—not so much against any inherent fault in that media, but because the media has been considered as a replacement to a valued friend: the book. Too often this attitude against the newer media has become more than a knee-jerk reaction, for there has been widespread disenchantment with nonprint media—media ballyhooed in messiahlike terms, which because of both inherent and utilization flaws could never meet advance notices.

But in the learning center as an integrated, fully coordinated facility, all media and their functions can be combined to meet the educational demands of the patron. Though the learning center should be able to eliminate the dichotomous philosophical split between print and nonprint professionals, it is important to understand how these various philosophical postures are "naturally" developed.

Instructional media and library science have long held parallel and sometimes overlapping positions within education; specialists in both are concerned with the control and management of media, have generally received training in graduate level schools, and in function have had primarily nonteaching roles. Because of financial restraints, administrators in schools often have chosen personnel capable of functioning in relation to both print and nonprint media. Personnel in print and nonprint areas also have been closely associated with the software and hardware industries. Hence both professionals have coordinate fields of postgraduate employment in business, and both professions have regular nonschool areas of employment with the government, the public, and industry.

The acceptance of integration which then provides all media resources to meet patron needs in the learning center should be based on several premises.

1. Media, regardless of their formats, should be viewed first for their informational and stimulus possibilities and second for their format potentials.

2. Schools do not provide learning but an access to learning. The instructor is an engineer of learning environments, a manager of information, and a learning counselor.

3. Media extends an instructor, both buoying up his instruction and enlarging that instruction. At times, mediation may provide a peripheral and/or reinforcing stimulus and at other times it may provide all of the instruction.

4. Learning and instruction are not one and the same. A school provides for learning, and instruction is but one element in the learning milieu.

5. The wide variety in type and emphasis of stimulus media should be developed to maximize learning potentials. The multiplicity of educational goals and goal paths must be provided for through a plurality of stimuli.

6. An integrated approach to learning is most economical in terms of all human and non-human resources.

7. Though education is at best an imprecise "science," a technology of instruction is now becoming available and that technology can best be introduced through a learning center.

A Library

With such an integrative approach, the major internal change is an attitudinal one. *The* library becomes *a* library within *the* learning center. Though the resources available will probably be far more extensive than before, there may well be an initial feeling that the library has been de-emphasized. The truth is, of course, that the needs of the learner have been emphasized and each function, including the library, has become strengthened and more important.

In the center, all previous library functions are maintained

25

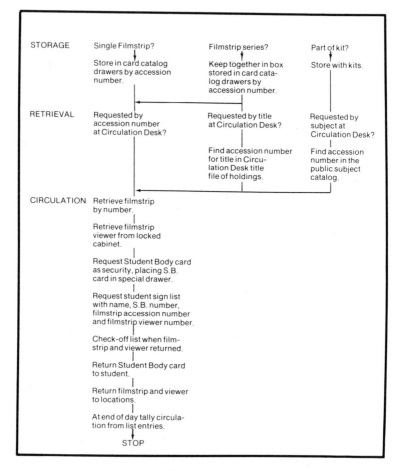

Figure IV

though the breadth of them will probably be enlarged. Thus the librarian with an expertise in information description, storage, retrieval, and circulation, will be concerned with all media. For instance, figure IV shows how a librarian in a newly developed learning center used analytical skills to solve the problem of establishing storage space, security, and circulation procedures for filmstrips.

An excellent description of how the library has evolved into the learning center and how that library can be described within the concept has been developed by Lyndon Vivrette, Head Librarian and Learning Center Director of Cuesta College. The following quotation is from an unpublished brochure, *Learning Center Unlimited*, 1974.

The Philosophy

The Learning Center will totally support each educational instruction method of each instructor, meet the separate and individual learning and study needs of each student, and will provide cultural and educational resource opportunities to the community.

The facility is to be a TRADITIONAL LIBRARY with total media storage and retrieval capability without distorting the image or function of the traditional library.

The emphasis will be placed on meeting the unique needs of the individual user. The facility will adapt to the individual instead of forcing the individual to adapt to the facility. This interior flexibility must be capable of continual change and expansion, accomplished conveniently and routinely.

It is essential that this facility be capable of adapting to any existing or future instructional media or technology with a minimum of effort or cost. The center will continually explore and experiment with new technology and systems of support for instruction and provide the facilities for these innovations.

The overall environment will aggressively display materials and resources in an attractive and subtle manner that does not disturb the traditional aesthetics.

The facility will provide individual learning equipment and study space, and is to be staffed with librarians who have attained state teaching credentials in order to support the instructors' and the students' goals.

Capability for communications from any distribution point to all students in any area, with connections to all furniture and equipment within the facility, to each classroom, to every building on campus, and to the outdoor landscaped areas on the campus grounds will be integrated into the design of the facility. The interior environment will be capable of supporting all activities and will have adjustable controls for lighting, ambient sound, and air movement within the facility as it is required. All air space surfaces above the human level will be capable of multi-screen projection.

The interior components, equipment and furniture will be of a small modular design with the capability for reassignment of unit function and for immediate rearrangement of all floor spaces.

The interior architecture will be so planned as to permit maximum efficiency with minimal staffing and minimal requirement for security controls.

The question as to how a library as part of the learning center can better meet changing needs is not clearly answerable. Certainly since "library" and "media" are generic terms and services, the providing of information in multiformats constitutes a more comprehensive approach. As more and varied patrons enter the center for its variety of services, needs can be ascertained more readily. As education continues to serve ever new markets, masses which had been defined as the culturally disadvantaged or different could become the center's majority users. Then, the library function could become the prime way to return power to the people, for information is power.

Audiovisual Services

". . . the term audio-visual instructional materials is liberally interpreted to comprise the many substances and sounds which play important roles in teaching and learning. These are the realities of things that are seen, heard, felt, smelled, manipulated, organized, assembled, or taken apart during learning; they are the things that are ultimately labeled, talked about, criticized, or praised, read about, or thought about during learning; and they are the things that are remembered, recalled pleasurably, or used and re-used after learning." (Brown, James W., Lewis, Richard B., and

Harcleroad, Fred F. *A-V Instruction Materials and Methods.* McGraw Hill Book Company, 1964. p. vii.)

Though that definition is as comprehensive as one could be, for the purposes of this discussion, the merits of "AV" will not be given a great deal of space. Rather, we are here interested in the development of AV services and how they add to the total service concept of the learning center. And though AV services are to be defined as hardware support, nonprint media, media utilization techniques, and the local production of instructional media, a short history of the movement is provided here so that an understanding of this important part of the learning center will be complete.

When "AV" became important enough to be written about, the predominant way of considering it was to view media as an aid to instruction. The preoccupation at that stage was for the machines, techniques, and materials which made instruction more interesting, extending the instructor in a variety of ways. The unique contribution of media was the defining argument the AV advocate used to make inroads into the verbal literacy of the lecturer with textbook in hand. In this early stage of development, little consideration was made for the individual and his needs. Programmed instruction was not yet important; rather, the presentation of a lot of information to a lot of people predeominated the movement.

Certainly during this period of time Edgar Dale's "Cone of Experience" was the great influencing model for AV innovators. In that model Dale presented a theoretical continuum of experiences from the direct, purposeful experience on one end to verbal symbols on the other. Though this model was valuable when discussing types of learning situations and experiences, it tended to focus too heavily on the messages' forms rather than on the individual's needs and how the messages' forms and content affected him. Furthermore, advocates of the model dichotomized the elements so much that verbal symbols were viewed as being almost "bad" and the multiform approach (all media, experiences, and avenues of presentation and feedback) to instruction was badly weakened. "Film was good and lecture was bad." Unfortunately the old style AV advocate is still interested in pushing film and the overhead projector. Too often, he does that—including pushing the equipment to the classroom.

Along with this movement of providing audiovisual media in instructional situations, the need for better, more highly tailored media became apparent. "Communication" became a key in educational conversation and the medium indeed began to be looked upon as the message. This close tie-in between the medium and the message in the communication-conscious society led to the local production movement.

Though the local production movement did not exclude such media as those for the tactile and auditory senses, the prime, almost exclusive, form of expression was the visual. There was and is abundant evidence that in general the best instruction or learning comes from a combination of audio and visual messages while the least effective is the audio only (as in a lecture!). Thus, the concentration of the local production movement was on providing the individual teacher with a way to produce a visual image which he had designed himself and which met his exact learning specifications.

Once large amounts of locally produced or commercially prepared media began to be used in the classroom, the AV movement began emphasizing techniques. The instructor standing between an overhead projector and the screen, projecting a shadow of his head rather than a message was and is all too clear an image in our recollections. Thus, classes on the utilization of media became important parts of teacher training programs and as in-service components of faculty development programs.

Gradually these technique classes started to consider individualized and individual learning strategies. At that point, with the behavioral orientation becoming strong, a technology of instruction began to surface and the instructional development movement began to take hold.

So long as the audiovisual/instructional media movement was loose, trying on its own to improve instruction and build its own resources, its competitive posture created problems in education. The educational dollar was limited and the AV proponent was looked upon as an empire builder whose almost monocular view of what was right in education created proponents and enemies. Within the learning center movement, the competitive nature is reduced and the AV resources of media, hardware, production, and a utilization technology are strengthened and delivered as a more comprehensive service for the student and the faculty member.

This inclusion of "AV" in a "library-like" atmosphere is not as unusual as some might assume.

> . . . The incorporation of media materials in the library and the development of learning or instructional resource centre activities raises the question of the nature of the relationship of the library to the means of media production. Increasingly the library has begun to act as an initiator of material to support the work of the institution it serves. Libraries have been accustomed to issue guides to their services, handbooks concerning the literature of various subjects, accession lists, catalogues, bibliographies and, more recently, current awareness services to match subject interest profiles. Photocopying and microfilming facilities have made such 'production' work very much simpler. Many libraries have also been concerned with the organization of exhibitions, the preparation and distribution of packages of educational material, and with identifying gaps in the literature of particular subjects and areas of study. Certain libraries have moved forward as media production facilities have become more simple to handle, producing tape-slide and film introductions to the library and to the use of the literature in various subject fields, and undoubtedly this will become more common as videocassettes and television cameras come into general use. Libraries will increasingly anticipate demands for material, influence methods of instruction, and 'publish' materials for various classes of library user. It has been suggested that running a resource centre is like running a public library except that you have to write and print and publish the books as well. (Enright, B. J. *New Media and the Library in Education.* Linnet Books & Clive Bingley, 1972. pp. 121-122.)

It was thus these two services—library and audiovisual activities—which had shared some enmity became the initial cohabitants of the early learning center.

II

The Concepts

*Instructional Development and Nontraditional
Services and Learning Activities*

Thus from the union of the traditional library and AV services a new institution, the learning center, developed. Now we shall see how that alliance produced instructional development and as a result of many factors a fourth service—non-traditional in nature—moved into the center's family of services.

Instructional Development

In considering the historical movement towards a learner-oriented center there is a clear transitional growth from heavy hardware support and some production to heavier production and finally to the place where both hardware and production support instructional development activity within the learning center.

But what is "instructional development" and why is there so much discussion of this "sudden giant" in educational circles?

Paul Saettler in his book *A History of Instructional Technology* (McGraw-Hill, 1968), gives us some insights as to how the AV movement spawned a technology of instruction—of

TRANSITIONAL GROWTH

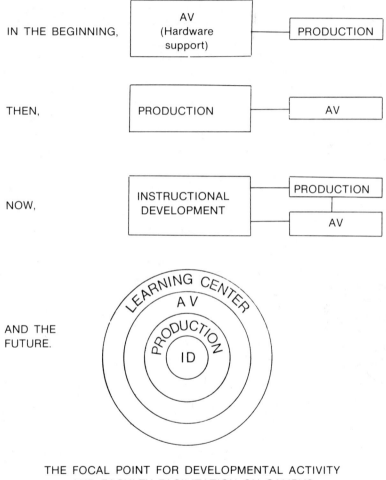

THE FOCAL POINT FOR DEVELOPMENTAL ACTIVITY
AND FACULTY FACILITATION ON CAMPUS

Figure V

which instructional development is its major actualizing agent.

During the early "Cone of Experience" history of instructional technology, Saettler sees the movement as dominated by a physical science concept (pp. 2-4); as we noted in the previous chapter, that period "seems to have been relatively little influenced by educational needs or psychological theory in relation to the design of instructional messages or experimental media research." (Saettler, p. 2).

> Today there is an emerging Zeitgeist that an applied behavioral science approach to the problems of learning and instruction is fundamental to instructional technology. Thus the basic view of the behavioral science concept of instructional technology is that educational practice should be more dependent on the methods of science as developed by behavioral scientists in the broad areas of psychology, anthropology, sociology, and in the more specialized areas of learning, group processes, language, and linguistics, communications, administration, cybernetics, perception, and psychometrics. Moreover, this concept includes the application of engineering research and development (including human factors engineering) and branches of economics and logistics related to the effective utilization of instructional personnel, buildings (learning spaces), and such new computerized machine systems as data processing and information retrieval. (Saettler, p. 5).

Though instructional development (ID) grew out of the AV movement, it is more than an extension of that of movement. The author in a presentation before the joint state conference of the California Association of School Librarians and the California Association of Educational Media and Technology in 1972 defined ID as a process, the focusing of a team of specialists (subject matter, learning, media, management, production, evaluation, etc.) on the task of analyzing the components (audience, task, environments, etc.) of a learning system in order to meet specific objectives through the selection, production, sequencing, engineering, and testing of that which may make up a learning environment. He strongly suggested ID as the only way to make a significant change in the learning potential of education as we know it.

The components of the instructional development process leading to the brash conclusion of that statement should indicate the reason why this emerging giant has become a central part of the learning center. But before launching into a discussion of the elements of the instructional development process, it seems appropriate to consider the major agents of our times—systems and applied learning theory—which the author believes have created the opportunity ID provides us.

Systems

Management of resources, and the recognition that *knowledge* of all that makes up a unit (or system) leads to potentially better management, resulted in the rise of analytic approaches of operations research, model building, computer simulations, and electronic data processing. Systems approaches which approached human nature problems (man/worker/student interacting with numerous variables within a system) and attempted to optimize output in fiscal terms obviously took hold quickly in the business world. But as the financial crunch bore down on us in education, we began to utilize economic analysis techniques to determine whose resources were being spent in our own system or systems. Just now, that technique is beginning to gain real acceptance from those who are concerned with the essence of education—instruction. And though much has not yet been done to determine which sets of learning strategies are most cost effective/cost beneficial (it could be determined which system leading to output A is the cheapest), we are interested in applying management tools to determine which variables exist in the learning system and how learning can be optimized.

Certainly within the systems approach in education one man, Dr. Robert Mager, stands alone as the major influence in the field. Mager's approach was simply to put on record demonstrable (identifiable) objectives (resulting in "outputs" in the systems jargon) from which instructional systems could be designed and *evaluated*. And though Dr. Mager has been regularly praised and criticized for this "simplistic" approach to instructional planning, there can be no doubt that both the most astute, master teacher and the novice intern can improve their teaching if they would only consider and then apply some of Dr. Mager's principles, principles which would elucidate learners needs and then determine if those needs had been met through competency-based instructional systems.

Applied Learning Theory

Even as systems models gave us ways to analyze the constituents of learning situations, educational researchers have discovered enough about the human learner and the learning task to allow educators make significant changes in those educational situations. And yet educators have not applied this knowledge to any great extent. Why? Perhaps we are at the threshold of radical changes! Learning theory is no longer theory if it can become law through research and application. But even the research and development centers of less than a decade ago did not make any significant changes in education. It is puzzling: we have knowledge and yet we do not use it. Certainly professional preparation programs do not prepare teachers to use this newer knowledge on learning. Gagne's *The Conditions of Learning (Holt, Rinehart, and Winston, Inc., 1965)* which compiles a good deal of that which we know about learning could be applied if there were agents in our schools who would aid the teacher in developing their instructional sequences.

So we have the powerful tools of systems and the knowledge of a learning theory/research which can be applied now. These are the tools of the instructional developer; these are the challenges and opportunities of instructional development. The developer should be able to improve instruction significantly. Acting within the structure of the learning center, he will be able to do so through established organizational patterns, for the center's faculty patron now has material resources and personnel services for direct assistance in instruction. The limitation of resource use to only supplement and complement instruction as in media resource programs of the past is outdated.

The complex instructional development model presented in figure VI provides the three major tracks or areas of instructional development: analysis; snythesis; evaluation and applica-

UNIT OF INSTRUCTION

SIMPLIFIED INSTRUCTIONAL DEVELOPMENT PROCESS

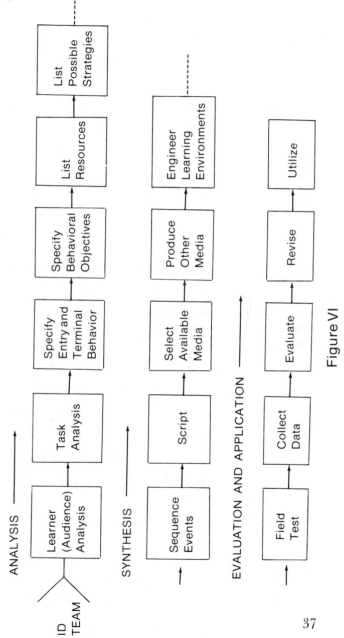

Figure VI

tion. The instructional developer working with the teacher and the other learning specialists must guide the team through these tracks.

Since it is not the purpose of this book to elaborate completely on all that is part of the LC, no deep discussion of ID can be made here. However, a quick examination of some of the the newer, more intricate ingredients of ID will help in selecting professionals capable of expediting the process.

Learner Analysis. As many characteristics as possible of each learner in the learning situation must be determined so that decisions can be made as to strategies for instruction. If we know, for instance, that individual "A" functions most effectively in the morning, learns best from ikonic visuals, is reinforced best by verbal praise, etc., etc., we will better be able to provide strategies and environments for him." Usually, the problem is to identify the major characteristics of a large audience and then provide instruction which fits the needs of the majority, but including options for an individual to satisfy specific needs. Learner analysis is difficult (persons wishing to learn about more about it should read material on "cognitive mapping") and at this time is an infant in its own development.

Task Analysis. When we know a good deal about the learners in an instructional situation, we should be ready to define the prerequisites and conditions needed for something to be learned. Here, Gagne's work is invaluable. If we decide that the learning task is concept formation, Gagne would tell us that concept learning allows us to respond to things and events as a class. He would then tell us (p. 134-35) to look for the following conditions:

> Conditions within the Learner: Prerequisites to the learning of concepts are capabilities that have previously been established by mutliple discrimination. A set of verbal (or other) chains must have previously been acquired to representative stimulus situations that exhibit the characteristics of the class that describes the concept and that distinguish these stimuli from others not included in the class . . .
>
> Conditions within the Situation: In human learners, the situational conditions for learning concepts are largely

embodied in a set of verbal instructions . . .

1. The specific stimulus objects . . . are presented simultaneously, or in close time succession . . .

2. Instructions go on to elicit the same common link to a stimulus situation belonging to the proper class but to which the learner has not previously responded . . .

3. Once these events have occurred, the new capability may be verified by asking for the identification of several additional instances of the class, again using stimuli to which the learner has not acquired specific verbal chains. If these are successfully done, one may conclude that a new concept has been learned.

There is a great deal more to the learning of a concept and its reinforcement against forgetting. However, providing conditions for that task (as described by Gagne) will optimize the opportunity to learn. In the ID process, this knowledge of learning theory can become a powerful tool.

The specification of objectives, strategy, resource selection and development, and sequencing of events should follow learner and task analysis. What instructional development has done, then, is to delay decision making on instructional strategies until information has been collected about the learner, outcomes have been specified, and tasks analyzed. How much better this is than the regular way of first selecting a textbook and then doing something about planning for the course. Imagine the absurd situation of a teacher selecting a textbook for a class and then arriving on the first day to find that all the members of the class are blind. A little learner analysis would have avoided that and putting off the decision on a textbook might have freed up decisions on learning strategies. Too often the text dictates what happens in a class; the teacher is supposed to be the manager of the learning environment.

The ID process can indeed end with the developed learning unit. However, if what has been developed is to be valid, it must be checked (tested) to see if it is effective. Thus, evaluation and application should follow development. By strenuously following such a regimen, strategies will be strong and there will be a high "chance" of success.

But instructional development can follow very simple models

PLANNING AND PRODUCING INSTRUCTIONAL MEDIA

I. Planning
   A. The big idea (a problem to solve?)
   B. Objective statements (purposes—to solve the problem?)
   C. Conditions for the presentation
      1. Audience
      2. Environment
      3. Available hardware
      4. Available software
      5. Available time for presentation
   D. Resources for production (Equipment, raw stock, etc.)
   E. Brainstorming alternatives
      1. Possible content
      2. Attendant media
      3. Follow-up activities
      4. Introducing the presentation (how do you do it?)
      5. Best length for presentation
      6. Etc.
   F. Content outline (try to put in temporal order)
   G. Storyboard (expanding the content)
   H. Scripting
   I. Transitions (putting in the verbal and musical elements to hold media together

II. Producing
   A. Scheduling the events
   B. Capturing the content (picture taking, audio recording in the field, etc.)
   C. Editing (matching script and storyboard)
   D. Captioning additional content, if needed
   E. Questions
      1. Is the organization logical?
      2. Is the story line complete?
      3. Is the presentation too long? too short?
      4. Are you satisfied at this point?
      5. Are you meeting your objectives?
   F. Preparation of captions and titles
   G. Coordination of media
      1. Preparation of audio
      2. Synchronization of audio, visual, print, etc.

III. Evaluating
   A. Field test
   B. Revise
   C. Utilize
   D. Revise?

Figure VII

also. The chances are high that the instructional developer will work more with instructors whose classes have already been offered numerous times before. The class will not be completely redone. Rather, small parts of it will be carefully, under tight time constraints, redone. Take the development of class objectives, for instance. The teacher might look at the results of the final exams of classes he has given before. If seventy-five percent of the people demonstrated that they understood concept "A," wouldn't it be expected that this should be an objective of his instruction? So, to get this instructor into the ID process, the developer might help him write objectives from past exam questions. Then, the next time the class is offered, students will have a clear set of learning specifications written as behavioral objectives. *Voila*, instant development: truth in education—"you can expect to learn this . . . ." Logically then, when time was available, the instructor would analyze the objectives, removing the inappropriate ones and their strategies and adding more desirable ones.

The instructional development service as a systematic process changes media services. Under a traditional plan for media service the decisions for instructional planning are made by the individual teacher who may or may not seek support from media. Thus, traditionally, the service role for media is a general one in which direction for activities and purchasing must be made with a "crystal ball" and follow principles of versatility and mobility. Such decisions are frequently inefficient and costly to both the instructional process and to the budget. The process could be depicted as in figure VIII.

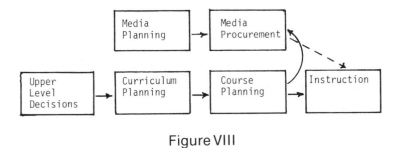

Figure VIII

While media planning and procurement should occur no later than at the curriculum level (and probably earlier) and be connected with it, usually parallel systems exist which only tangentially affect each other at a level where major decisions have already been completed in both systems.

Under the behaviorally oriented instructional development program, systems are not self-reliant. Decisions are made which affect instruction in a direct manner. Using a basic paradigm of which any subsystem can be evaluated and/or redesigned, the course of instructional planning follows an orderly, *visible*, procedural path.

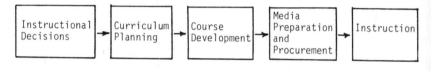

| Instructional Decisions | → | Curriculum Planning | → | Course Development | → | Media Preparation and Procurement | → | Instruction |

Figure IX

As an example of the two systems, let us construct an hypothetical situation which could exist under either system.

Situation. School X is teaching six sections of "bonehead" English each semester. About 240 students are enrolled each semester.

Media Services Outside the Instructional Process Through An Availability Center. The department hires teaching assistants (T.A.) to teach four of the sections. Two are taught by new faculty members with doctorates. The media center upon being informed of the classes purchases a small collection of Harvard Reading Films, some sample copies of programmed texts, and a few filmstrips on writing, library usage, etc. Since it is not known who will be teaching the classes each semester, the media list is sent to the department head who will pass on copies to the appropriate instructors. The semester begins; there are six classes of forty students each. Professor X would prefer to be teaching "Milton's Aereopagitica: TheUltimate Argument against Censorship"! T.A. number two is working on his dissertation and so overlooks much of his mail, including the media list. The classes are taught in various buildings and at various times. Professor Y has never met T.A. number one but they both plan on using the Harvard Reading Films for the first three weeks of class. T.A. number one's class starts ten minutes after Professor Y's finishes. Sometimes the film and projector make it between classes on time. Once the equipment breaks down due to its untimely dumping in a snow drift as it is being pushed between classes. *Result*: uneven, nonevaluatable messages which overtax the flow channel's capacity; poorer quality media signals (e.g. less specific media displayed on equipment whose quality has been sacrificed for portability).

Media Service as a Part of an Instructional Development System. The administration is concerned that the best possible instruction be provided students. Because of the problems "bonehead" English students have exhibited in classes taken subsequent to their "bonehead" class, a better instructional process must be developed. The Instructional Planning Committee is given the task of planning the proper strategy for educating the group. Since this is a most important task, the best instructor, Professor Z, is asked to serve as a consultant and to consider the possibility of teaching this group of students. Because there are a large number of students, and because it is decided that much of the work for such a class is both sedentary and individual, it is decided that students will receive one lecture unit of instruction per week. The rest of the time will be devoted to individual counseling and to the use of appropriate mediated instruction. Professor Z as a part of a team prepares a set of lessons which are put on video tape. Lessons are distributed to available classrooms several times a week and to the dormitories several nights a week. Eight-mm reading films are prepared from 16-mm copies and study carrels are outfitted in the learning center (which is open seven days a week). Assigned papers are read by T.A.s who record comments on tapes which are then put into the center with the papers and which may then be checked out by students. Regular small group study programs are set up with T.A.s. *Result*: a high quality, definable and evaluatable instructional signal.

In each situation students are given a particular instructional message. The quality of the stimulus and its appropriateness varies considerably in the two approaches. In the system's approach, media service fills a consultant's role in planning and then acts as a supplier of a high quality signal in a variety of situations. In the availability approach supplementary services only are provided.

Let us consider examples of two categories of the development function as a service paradigm: the information function and the operational or activity function. The first, the information function, includes consultation activity, methodology (through service courses, individual counseling, etc.), and media and service information (through manuals, memos, bibliographies, sample libraries, etc.). The second, the operational function, deals with production and the management and distribution of message signals. This second function is the natural consequence of the first. The resultant outputs or consequences of such a system would then be new and better learning environments, improved instruction, improved efficiency in information distribution, instruction-related media, and possible cost benefits.

The paradigm can be used as an approach for problem solving (student dissatisfaction with instruction, faculty dissatisfaction with resource availability, shortage of funds, and a need for greater inservice training of professional mediators) in which there would be a reassignment of some of the faculty, the provision of efficient and less costly means for dealing with larger student numbers, and the improvement of learning environments.

Instructional development then functions in a number of ways and for both classroom instruction and individual and individualized instruction. Within the learning center it provides a way to develop independent courses of study, mini-courses, peripheral media to support regular classroom instruction (but within the center), etc. In the larger environment of the school, the ID process provides instructors with ways of updating present courses and of developing new ones.

Nontraditional Services and Learning Activities

One of the major contributions any learning center can make to its institution is the provision of spaces for the experimentation with, and development of, a number of activities which might not easily find homes under other organizational auspices on campus. It is important that some organization in the institution have such a role, and the learning center may well be that organization.

For brevity's sake, "nontraditional" education is defined loosely as learning activity outside of the classroom and the extension of such activity toward a fuller educational opportunity for all. There are several simpler reasons for the learning center to assume some of the activities and services which will be enumerated. First, since most learning centers will have originally been developed as libraries, the space available for normal library routines may be considered excessive by some. Thus, when space is sought for new activities, the LC's space will often be considered. Second, the extended hours of a learning center make it a natural province for many activities with varied time needs. "If the building is already open for other activities, why shouldn't it be used for this new activity?" is a question which will likely be asked. Third, the administrative expertise of LC personnel and the availability of that type of time (without the normal educational constraints of meeting class schedules) increases the chances that new roles—especially in developing new services—will be thrust upon such personnel.

Beside these reasons of space, time, and personnel, there is another reason why the development of nontraditional education has almost by fiat been thrust upon the learning center. Most educators agree that new services are needed, and since someone needs to take the lead in developing them, anyone willing to assume the developmental roles may have them!

What are some of the nontraditional learning services and activities which may occur in a learning center? Because of the experimental, innovative nature of the learning center, the concept of the LC does not indicate that all or even any of the services and activities might occur in any center. What should be found in the center are those programs which the school has

45

defined as being appropriate for it and for which it has granted priorities and hence resources. The center is thus a truly responsive part of the school.

Some examples of various types of nontraditional educational services for the student and for the faculty follow.

For the Student

The learning disability program and its euphemistic organizational name, the *Educational Diagnostic Clinic,* can be one of the most important new services in any school. At De Anza College with its "first-ever" clinic, Judy Triana described this program as follows.

The Educational Diagnostic Clinic is a program for students who have average or above average intellectual potential (as determined by standard tests of IQ) but who have specific learning disabilities (as determined by individual tests of learning abilities), and who are not functioning in the college program according to minimal standards. The program offers two areas of service: diagnostic testing and observation, and prescriptive teaching.

Each student is individually assessed in two general areas: (1) reception (comprehension), i.e., reading and listening, and (2) performance, i.e., writing and speaking His abilities and disabilities, including those related to medical, psychological, educational and "cultural" or language backgrounds, are identified. A profile of abilities is obtained and compared to available age-level-expectation norms.

An assessment of the student's academic or vocational course of study at De Anza is made and a program of specific instructional and counseling techniques is recommended. The goals are to encourage the student's present pursuits or guide him to a more realistic career or vocation. Close cooperation with the instructional and student personnel staff is necessary in the consideration of the students program at De Anza.

The diagnostic process is one which depends largely on the needs of the student *as he sees them,* either from his reported difficulties in learning situations, or those discovered in the process of individual testing and tutorial contact. The student, tutor and instructor share the responsibility for the student's diagnosis and education.

In addition to close individual assistance from the instructor, each student is offered tutorial assistance in both group and individual situations, during which time these procedures are followed:

(1) The tutors utilize media (auditory, visual, tactile or dinesthetic or a combination of these) specially suited to the student's learning strength to teach the subject matter.

(2) The instructor guides the student to available materials on campus or else where which would be appropriate for his particular needs.

(3) The instructor and/or tutor provide training experiences to build the areas of weakness determined most necessary to minimal success in his academic or vocational program at De Anza.

The goal of these individual tutorial sessions is to help the student to "survive" through the recognition of what resources and skill he has and the utilization of these skills to cope with the academic or training demands.

The program is based on the premises that: (1) for some students, the learning situation and utilization of what is learned must be specially designed according to the skills he has brought with him; (2) given certain advantages (i.e., "average" intelligence, emotional maturity and motivation) he can learn despite his physical, emotional, perceptual, and cognitive deficits; (3) it is our responsibility to determine what his deficits and strengths are, and relate these to the demands of a college education and provide learning experiences suited to his strengths; (4) the "learning to learn" concept is an important by-product of the experience; (5) for exceptional students, relevant and adequate teaching cannot proceed without information derived from testing and observation.

We have determined the test-then-teach method as being more efficient in determining which skill to teach first. It answers more specifically the "shy" of a problem which in turn suggests the order of the skills to be taught.

The goals of the program in general are to help the student survive in whatever area of study he has chosen and to guide the student to a more realistic area of study if his chosen area is incompatible with his skills.

By plan the De Anza clinic offers services to those of average or above average IQ. Because of limited resources, this was a way to maximize the payoff of resources expended through the clinic. As more and more educational administrators recognize that such funds are small in comparison to the human potential which can be realized through such programs, greater support and hence greater services should be expected.

Two case studies indicating the types of EDC patrons and strategies follow:

CASE STUDY No. 1
ERIC

Eric is a young man of twenty who was referred to the Educational Diagnostic Clinic by both his counselor and reading instructor. During our first interview, Eric expressed that his weaknesses were in the areas of reading, writing, and spelling. He also revealed that he has always been in special classes beginning from the fourth grade. At one point, he was receiving psychiatric counselling, which Eric felt, did not alleviate his learning difficulties. He appeared to be a bright young man, who expressed his ideas well verbally. Although putting on an air of confidence, he seemed nervous. This was evidenced by an occasional quivering in his voice and shaking in his hands.

Through a general achievement test, Eric indicated a good potential for learning. He also scored high on the reading comprehension subtest because visual clues were presented. His low areas were spelling and reading recognition.

We began to work with Eric in improving his reading skills. Through observation, we found adequate sound-symbol association skills with occasional visual reversal difficulties. However, his pace was slow and taxing. He reads phonetically, as his auditory channel in his strong mode of learning. Weaknesses in his visual modality are evident in his reading.

EDUCATIONAL DIAGNOSTIC
CLINIC PROGRAM

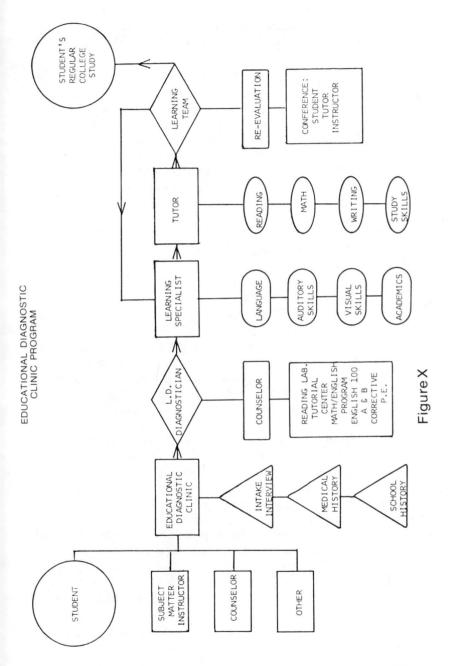

Figure X

Eric prefers to read his English assignments instead of hearing them on tape as he feels he must continue to practice reading to improve. Although he reads word by word, his comprehension is good. He can extract main ideas and retain details. He shows good ideas in his written expression. Sophisticated analogies are presented in his themes as well as pertinent examples. His spelling is poor as he spells everything as it sounds. This is, again, evidence of his strength in his auditory channel and weakness in his visual.

Eric continues to be tardy for appointments but is beginning to develop responsibility in meeting them. He is willing to accept help and has become less defensive about his disability.

CASE STUDY No. 2
KEVIN

Kevin is a young man with problems. Besides a history of epilepsy, he has also lost use of one of his arms as a result of an accident. These difficulties require him to be under constant medication. Kevin appeared as a sullen and angry young man when first interviewed. Medical, educational, and psychological information obtained indicates that general intelligence is not impaired. However, very specific learning disabilities are present. He enrolled in six regular classes, including academic subjects, physical education, and guidance but frequently did not attend them.

After conversations and an initial evaluation of Kevin, it was readily apparent that the learning modality most affected was the visual channel. Reading was a slow and laborious process for him and development in this area was severely impaired. Rather than concentrate on remediation of these reading difficulties, the Educational Diagnostic Clinic chose to utilize his strongest learning modality—the auditory channel. Tests of both auditory and visual abilities confirmed what we expected: that if Kevin compensated for his inability to handle visual symbols by using good listening skills; through these he could gain information faster and more efficiently. Once the input was made through the auditory channel, Kevin improved rapidly. However, the pace of learning was slow because of medically related problems.

How did Kevin best demonstrate what he had learned? Although his speech was slow and sometimes hesitant, the thoughts expressed were contextually adequate. Writing skills were also poor because of fine motor coordination difficulties. Despite this, his writing was legible, and so he was encouraged to further develop this mode of expression.

The Learning Specialist selected the following individualized program based on the preceding evaluation and utilizing Kevin's strong areas. Auditory input was made available through taped presentations of reading assignments. Kevin had to bring his text in each day so that taping could be done. Although we felt that this was a burden on him, and inefficient as well, it proved to have a positive effect on Kevin's attitude and motivation. He became very responsible and consistent in bringing his books and studying of the tapes. He found a way of learning which, for him, was more efficient and rewarding.

While involved in the Educational Diagnostic Clinic, Kevin was also receiving corrective P.E. instruction, counseling support and social stimulation from his peers. He passed all courses with fair grades, except for one academic subject which he was determined to make up during the following quarter. He was assigned a tutor during the summer and fall quarters. Latest reports from his instructors and tutor reveal that he is progressing at a good rate. He is perceived by those involved with his program at De Anza as a more responsible and motivated student. His social encounters are seen as frequent and positive.

What is the next step for Kevin? We feel that his efforts must lead to a vocation which would make him at least partially independent. This long term goal, we feel, would help sustain him through rigorous demands of a college education. We are not suggesting that Kevin's learning problems are over, nor that he could not have achieved the same degree of success in a similar program. However, it is important to realize that learning problems are not unique to the elementary and secondary schools. Specialists must be available to recognize and help the student also at the college level.

* * *

The placement of a diagnostic clinic within the learning center has a number of advantages. First, the clinic can utilize the open media lab and its many resources. Second, the clinic is operationally located close to instructional development services which can be utilized in developing strategies and materials needed by the learning handicapped student. Third, the learning specialist in the clinic can serve as a learning expert on the instructional development team. The specialist's knowledge of the individual learner, learning modalities, and the conditions of learning will be invaluable during the instructional development process. Fourth, because the clinic is located within a total center for learning it may avoid some of the stigma such a learning disability program still seems to have. Finally, the clinic can readily take advantage of other learning resources in the center such as learning materials and the tutorial program.

The Tutorial Program exists to support all students in the school. In many schools, splinter efforts exist for various small groups, but a unified program for all students provides a greater opportunity for success.

The tutorial program can serve in a number of ways:

1. Tutoring within classes. This activity provides laboratory-like experiences in which the teacher and assistants act as tutors to individuals and small groups. Though such classes as math appear most obvious for such services, almost any class from psychology to computer technology, from "bonehead" English to instrumental music can be improved through tutorial activities.

2. Tutoring individuals and small groups. Individuals with the same problem (as, for instance, learning to do quadratic equations), whether from one class or several classes, and/or those needing special help outside of a formal class (e.g., an individual may wish to learn to play a musical instrument which is not taught at that school) can receive help.

3. Tutoring services for special group or individual needs. Tutors may be used to provide educational assistance for those in such programs as the educational diagnostic clinic, those using independent studies but who need human help, etc.

Once resources for such a program have been allocated, three major things must be done to provide a successful service. First, an administrative structure is needed which clearly defines the parameters of services and the mechanisms to be used to provide that service. Where will tutoring occur? How do you find tutors? How are tutors paid? How are tutorial services to be evaluated and updated?

Second, a highly defined but flexible program is required for involving faculty in the planning and utilization of the service. How can the teacher be persuaded to have his students utilize the tutorial program?

Third, a quality program for the selection and training of tutors must be developed. Peer tutors must have subject expertise, have the operational tools to demonstrate both process and knowledge to the tutee, and know how to move the tutees through the difficult process of learning.

Independent Studies. As group-oriented instruction gave way to individualization, many forms of instruction and even more labels for them began to permeate the literature. Independent studies, mini-courses, individual learning modules, personalized instruction, individualized instruction, self-directed learning, etc.—all describe what we shall call independent studies. For the purpose of this discussion, independent study is meant to refer to an individual who initiates, pursues, and concludes some study which can be undertaken without the help of teacher or tutor. It does not include computer-aided instruction which is described elsewhere.

Independent study has the advantages of self-pacing, utilization of times best for the individual, etc. Within an open media lab and with the opportunity to provide tutorial help, the independent study program of the learning center can provide a useful adjunct to the rest of the academic climate of the institution. Packaged instruction should be given close scrutiny.

The following questions should help:

1. How does one provide the *necessary reinforcement* so that the learner will continue with the instruction? Certainly one of the major problems with programmed texts has been that immediate knowledge of correct response has not continued long as a reinforcer. Even when large steps and different schedules of reinforcement are introduced, many individuals will quickly tire of the instructional mode. Yet packaged learning as individual learning should seek to provide for individual dif-

ferences. Every package of instruction must have either a linearity or branching characteristic, and that sequencing can not be completely didactic.

2. When is *human intervention* important? And when it is important, do authors build it in as a function of a learning model which represents the basic conditions for learning? Intervention models may be built either so that the learner activates second person involvement or so that intervention is provided on a temporal basis. Ideally, a package could provide both a panic button and a regular opportunity for person-to-person involvement.

3. Are many packages too *heavily hardware-based*? As we move away from the greatest product of technology—the book —will the available hardware provide too much format direction? Will we, for instance, decide that since a wet carrel with a slide projector and cassette recorder is available, instruction should be put in the form of slides and tape? Certainly, we should be working from task and learner analysis developmentally before any format is determined.

4. How does this form of instruction affect the type of funding available to maintain the program?

5. *How does one administer a package?* It may be part of a course or it may be a total course. Are educators prepared and are manufacturers competent engineers?

6. Will there be an *overemphasis on individual learning* packages to the detriment of small group interactive packages? It may be easier to design such activity for one individual, but engineering for groups may in many cases produce more and better learning. With an emphasis on individualized instruction, will too many think that the individual can not be properly treated as a member of a group?

7. *Lock-step sequencing* is a problem in the traditional classroom. It can be an even greater one when packaged. How does one diminish the problem?

8. Are marketed products *behaviorally valid*? Learning psychologists can tell us much about the learner and the learning task, but has anyone effectively translated research into usable learning formulas? A technology of education may be possible, but developmentally we are just beginning to produce testable models of instruction.

9. *Have packages been validated with large numbers of people?* Are we to continue to allow students to use untested products?

10. *Can we afford mediated instruction* when 80 to 85 percent of an educational budget may go for salaries? For instance, if Professor X, a famous subject matter specialist and master teacher, develops a learning package costing $40,000, can we purchase it? Over a few years such a package may pay for itself by replacing personnel. But the replacement of the classroom teacher is an unthinkable proposition in our society.

11. Have authors of packages taken full advantage of *game formats* for learning packages? Some educators believe that simulation may one day be one of the most powerful learning tools used in education.

12. If packaged instruction really aims at individualizing instruction (and not just in putting it in a new format), shouldn't packages be designed so that *entrance can occur at various stages* within the total instructional sequence?

13. Learning has *cognitive, affective, and psychomotor components.* Though these all relate and are evident in most learning, the affective as a major component is difficult to measure and direct. Are packages appropriate for learning to appreciate or enjoy? Will we have sufficient expertise and time to evaluate affective development?

Though packaged instruction is not a panacea, there are strong reasons for giving it serious consideration. First, students are made more *responsible for their own progress.* Though this creates problems, it is an important and relevant consideration for educators.

Second, the *learner operates at his own pace*, making remediation less difficult. When, as an individual, he must return to again consider previously encountered media, he does not affect the pace of other learners nor does he develop inappropriate self-concepts because of peer notice.

Third, in the learning center, administrators of learning, not conventional instructors, may be used and entrance into a mini-course may occur when the student is psychologically prepared to start at the neginning of a semester or quarter, the last week of such a time unit, or during a vacation period.

Fourth, the act of learning during interaction with packaged material is *more visible and hence more evaluatable*. Certainly one of the factors which has retarded the improvement of instruction most is that it is difficult at best to evaluate a teacher in front of a class. But technology has made learning processors much more visible.

Fifth, one of the most positive aspects of packaged learning is that is *moves from a teacher-centered model to a learner-centered one*. If education as a system is to be improved, emphasis must be placed on that which is processed, the student.

Finally, packaged learning can overcome some of the unobtrusive but highly important *psychological factors* such as conceptual tempo which, working as an expectancy factor, inadvertently creates self-fulfilling prophecies which will act to the detriment of certain learners.

Along with mediated forms of independent study, *special projects* designed along independent lines can be offered. As an example, De Anza College's Learning Center special project class description may be useful in designing similar learning experiences.

Guidelines:

1. There will be one "teacher of record" each quarter; however, the student will choose one LC specialist who will guide his project. That specialist may well be someone other than the "teacher of record" who is listed in the schedule of classes.

2. The "teacher of record" will be responsible for turning in grades and doing other bookwork necessary for the course's operation.

3. The assignment of either one or two units of credit will be a function of the specialist and the student's appraisal of the project as to the following guideline:

    1 unit: 36 hours of conference, research, etc.

    2 units: 72 hours of conference, research, etc.

4. Activity Flow:

    a. Student locates LC specialist.

    b. Student and specialist redefine problem in general terms.

    c. Student and specialist determine if specialist is the most appropriate one for this problem. If not, a new LC specialist is located.

d. "Behavioral Objective" as a construct is defined and analyzed.
e. Behavioral objectives are written by student.
f. Conference held between student and specialist. Behavioral objectives are rewritten until appropriate.
g. Student and specialist discuss learning plans.
h. Plan is written by student.
i. Plan is evaluated by specialist. Plan is rewritten by student until specialist and student agree to its appropriateness.
j. Plan is implemented.
k. Progress meetings are held as appropriate.
l. Evaluation is made in terms of behavioral objectives.

The center may also offer quasi-independent study classes planned around its own resources. Since the center should offer alternative forms of instruction to those offered by the rest of the institution, the LC's only subject matter that is truly its own is that relating to its activities. Thus it may offer classes in the use of its library resources, in the development of instruction, in tutor training, etc.

Computer-Aided Instruction. A special form of independent study which may have a very large place in the learning center is computer-aided instruction in addition to other uses of the computer. John E. Coulson writing in *To Improve Learning* provided the following vivid description of the potential of computers.

Picture a college student of 1975, arriving at his study center in the morning and immediately sitting in front of a sophisticated console complete with tape recorder and earphones, slide and motion picture projectors, a television screen, a keyboard, and an electronic pen allowing free-hand student responses. This console, along with thousands of others on the campus, is connected to and controlled by a large central computer. The student receives instruction by means of multi-media presentations, and uses a variety of response modes to answer questions about the content material. The computer evaluates all responses and provides immediate corrective feedback. When the student needs further information to help him solve a problem, he communicates through the computer with a comprehensive automated library, typing his questions in normal English format and receiving immediate answers. He works entirely at his own pace and may see an entirely different sequence of material than any other student. With appropriate breaks for coffee and lunch, the student works in this individual manner until he is ready to go home in the afternoon.

The system just described is technologically feasible today. (Coulson, John E. "Computer-Assisted Instruction and Its Potential for Individualizing Instruction" in Tilson, Sidney G. *To Improve Learning*, volume 1, R. R. Bowker, 1970. p. 197.)

Though that picture has not yet been realized, the unique capabilities of the computer have a real place in the learning center. The computer can provide independent study (though in most places this will be very primitive in comparison to Coulson's description) and can be utilized as an information processor (even as a highly sophisticated calculator). The student of the near future will need to develop special computer skills in the same way learning to type has been considered an important skill in the past.

An open learning or media lab should be developed to provide a systematic hardware support system for many of the center's learning activities. Typically, such a laboratory supports the instructional program by providing space, equipment, and assistance for independent course work and for learning coordinated with regular classroom instruction. Usually wired carrels and computers handle all types of media. An open learning lab may contain the language lab and skills center media, and may support such programs as the tutorial and career centers, the diagnostic clinic, and independent studies.

Skills Program. The skills program accommodated by the open lab is an independent study service which many learning centers will wish to initiate. The program offers developmental work for students deficient in various learning skills but who may not have defined learning handicaps. Media in such a program will typically be available for remedial study in math, English, reading, writing, study techniques, etc.

As the total learning assistance program at the school and in the learning center continues to grow, the center may also become involved in coordinated efforts among reading and math labs, tutorial efforts, and learning disabilities programs. Such is the potential for the learning center. As an experimental area, a variety of programs can be tried. If they are found wanting they can be eliminated; if they are successes, they can be strengthened. Under this organizational structure, failure is to be occasionally expected, but no one is a loser and the student is always a winner.

Career Center. A final student service to be mentioned is the career center. This emerging program is a natural outgrowth of a society in which its members must plan for second, third, or even more careers. Today educational programs must be pointed in some way toward a career of some kind. Margaret Anstin, of De Anza College indicates the scope of the Learning Center's Career Center as follows:

> "Change" is the word of the times. Social, political and economic worlds turn topsy-turvy overnight. For students living in this world of daily crisis and unease there seems to be an overwhelming temptation not to plan their future at all. And yet, this decision to "make no decision at all" is just as binding as one carefully planned and adhered to concerning the future.
>
> In the past, persons were often thrust into jobs by chance or default, with little attempt to match their talents and aptitudes with work. Of that generation, statistics indicate 70% are now unhappy in their jobs. Today many of the old cliches regarding work are still in effect . . . . "A college education for everyone is the answer"; "Education for education's sake"; "work is its own reward." More and more students are rebelling against these biases and riding the pendulum in the opposite direction saying "Why work at all?" Somewhere in between can be found viable alternatives that tie "Education for living" in with "Education for earning a living."
>
> An essential part of education is its relation to the everyday world. For John Doe, that means the working world. Forty years of a man's life are spent preparing for and

pursuing his career and estimates indicate that he will shift career emphasis seven times in his lifetime. Can he leave this to chance?

Career Centers in high schools and colleges are entering the "no man's land" between education and work and attempting to bridge the gap. The purpose of the Career Center is to acquaint the student with the process involved in career selection and enable him to make informed choice as he prepares for his career. These choices hinge on the components of career development which include: knowledge of self, knowledge of work ethics, knowledge of career opportunities, knowledge of educational requirements and knowledge of the decision making process. Until recently the ability to integrate these components has been difficult because they were scattered. Part came through the counseling process, part through the library, and parts were often not touched on at all. The thrust behind a Career Center is to gather and focus the dimensions of career development around a central core—the resource center for researching the components. Once a Career Center is established and in readily usable form, the other components can flow into and from it in a continuous process.

Career counseling is the crux of sound career development. Whether individualized or in a class, such things as self assessment, values, work ethics and decision making are the building blocks of career choices.

There comes a time in the counseling process when the individual is ready to research literature on career clusters, A-V resources, and attend face-to-face interviews, seminars and "hands on" job experiences. The Career Center can centralize and facilitate the research and experiential part of career exploration.

Career development, then, is a process extending through life and involving the whole lifestyle of a person. The Career Center plus counseling offers the tools for making viable career decisions—including options and alternatives.

Nothing is certain these days except change, and the Career Center prepares persons to be ready and perhaps even welcome it.

There is no way to catalog all of the nontraditional services and activities which the learning center may offer the student. It takes no crystal ball, for instance, to see the center involved in directing external degree programs via both nonresidential study and non-traditional forms of instruction. Such a program might take advantage of independent studies, learning centers in the community, correspondence courses, and course work offered via newspapers, radio, TV, etc. It is exciting to consider the possibilities, and so long as the experimental, creative nature of the center can be maintained, such possibilities can become realities.

For the Faculty

While the majority of the learning center's activities directly support the student, the faculty member as a user of the center has a number of services available.

An office of *Institutional/Instructional Research and Grants* provides services, such as (1) conducting studies of academic and nonacademic programs in order to assist faculty and staff to evaluate, update, and improve the effectiveness of these programs; (2) conducting instructional research at the course level as part of the instructional development process in order to evaluate and update course objectives and strategies; (3) providing models and mechanisms for institutional evaluation; and (4) assisting the faculty in conceptualizing and writing proposals for funding from outside agencies.

A program such as a *learning center press* (somewhat along the lines of the small university press) can be developed to provide faculty and staff with a relatively inexpensive, easy to use service for the publication of print or nonprint media. While it should not be the purpose of such a press to provide for the publication of textbooks, political ideas, etc., a sharing of education-related ideas is important. With the aid of the LC print shop, the press can help develop staff and faculty by providing them with mass communication means to express ideas, and provide for institutional development by publishing research reports, proceedings of important meetings and conferences, etc.

While such a concept as that of the press may seem out of place and hard to visualize, its potential is enormous. It is easy, for instance, to imagine a regular program for the dissemination of the best new media developed by instructors working in the instructional development process. Under a profit-sharing plan, both the press (for its internal support along revolving fund lines) and its authors benefit, and instructional ideas are shared in a much larger educational circle.

As part of the sharing of ideas concept, the library service of the center may develop a *Selective Dissemination of Information Service* (SDI). With the vast amount of important information in books, pamphlets, magazines, newspapers and the newer media such as video being generated today, it becomes imperative that new means of communication (interfaces) be developed between the user and the information. Information is power, and in the educational institution such power is of paramount importance if the institution and its programs are to move forward.

The learning center as a regular service could optimize the information system by developing user profiles for all or a part of the faculty and administration. Through such a service, media is monitored on a regular basis; when matches with profiles needs are made, the information can be disseminated to the user. Since the faculty member has neither the tools of reference research nor the time and inclination for such research, this service should become a valued asset for the faculty and the school.

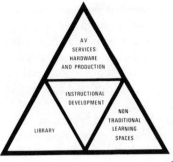

III

Setting Up the Center

Putting the Model Together

To reconstitute the concept before proceeding with its development, the model includes these four major parts: a library of media, audiovisual services, instructional development, and nontraditional services and learning spaces and activities. And though these parts have been discussed separately and in the order enumerated here, it should be clear that there is no clear delineation among the various parts, for they comingle, supporting each other; nor should a hierarchy of any kind exist. While the library and the learning resource center place their emphasis on resources (usually printed media), the learning center places its emphasis on learning—as both a product and a process. The learner and his special needs thus become central to the learning center's service, and no part of the model is less important than any other.

Learning Centers at Various Educational Levels

In the *elementary and primary schools* certain learning center concepts are more important than at any other level. A learning handicapped program begun at this level (and best as part of a national program!) could be the single most important learning assistance a school could provide. If cognitive, affective, and psychomotor handicaps are diagnosed early in educational life, the child can soon be returned to the educational mainstream (perhaps without ever leaving it), thus tasting success earlier and building on it so that this most important internal motivator will help bring success more quickly.

Although centers at this level may be limited by not having resources such as a fully funded and staffed library upon which to build the service, no learning center need be a grandiose organization. Initially, a simple service program supplying the hardware and software of instruction plus workshops on media utilization and strategy definition and development can be made available. As noted in an earlier chapter, once such a leadership role is established, new responsibilities and services are likely to follow if the center and its personnel are open and active.

Parenthetically, pre-school learning centers are beginning to be developed. The author has received reports on such centers in poorer rural and urban areas where a child is often stigmatized by a lack of intellectual experience when he or she enters the first grade or even kindergarten. Like a "Sesame Street" or "Electric Company", these pre-school learning centers provide vicarious experiences and intellectual stimulation so that the youngster can enter the educational mainstream immediately. Furthermore, such learning centers are not restricted necessarily to vicarious experiences. Field trips, speakers, realia, etc. can be be supplied to provide more variety and greater depth of learning.

In the *secondary school* learning centers as established entities are but a step away. Though certain high schools have highly developed centers, most are still at the multi-media or resource level. With strong library programs and heavy infusions of federal money for nonprint software and hardware, these service agencies have become very important in their schools.

The National Defense Education Act summer-and year-long institutes for the development of media specialists have also been extremely important for secondary institutions. Through these federally supported workshops and institutes a "new breed of cats" has been developed in the schools. These specialists, as former teachers and librarians, have the tools to provide a local production program, some strategy development, and an open system for the selection of both print and nonprint media for the educational experience.

Such centers are usually deficient in the areas of instructional development and nontraditional services. In the first instance, media personnel are available who can produce and demonstrate the utilization of that media. Such personnel, however, are not well trained in the areas of systems and learning psychology. Too often the school media specialist develops media without any clear plan for its use and no way to evaluate its effectiveness for either the individual or the group. But as instructional technology in academic programs replaces the more traditional audiovisual programs, new personnel and those returning for continuing education will receive the newer skills needed for instructional development.

In fact, the lack of nontraditional services may not be a deficiency in some schools. Since the nontraditional services offered should be those which the school deems appropriate, many such services exist elsewhere on the school campus. The wise administrator of the school will look at both the services which need to be provided and those which might be improved by being placed within the learning center.

The center in the *college and university* milieu is not easily quantifiable. In the newly developed community college center (the state of the art is discussed in a later chapter) with the emphasis of the college on good teaching, the center concept is taking firm hold. however, four-year colleges and universities have a unique problem. In most, the library is so strong, well-endowed, and often resistant to change that the other components of the LC model may have to be developed elsewhere on campus. Likewise, the AV services organization in the college is often already established in its own right. More and more such a service program is evolving along instructional development lines so that that service can also be provided. Likewise, strong counseling and student services programs are providing many of the learning assistance elements of the center concepts.

While centralization and decentralization each have merits

and problems, a number of institutions are breaking out of traditional decentralized molds and are now evolving along learning center lines. This break with tradition seems to be sparked by both financial and personnel considerations. Financial savings from centralization are only part of the reason, but with dwindling populations and hence fewer dollars to spend, school administrators are looking toward program development which will hold present students and attract new ones. Thus instructional development for better courses and independent studies, tutorial services, etc. promises much for the institution.

In addition a break with tradition by strong people in higher education who have embraced the concept and who are willing to accept the criticism for that break will do much to actualize the concept on campus.

Learning Centers Outside Formal Education

While major trends for learning center development are now being established in formal educational settings education on the periphery of formal instructional institutions is establishing its own versions of the concept. Take, for instance, this description by Robert W. Skinner, Major, United States Air Force, Chief, Wing Learning Center, Williams Air Force Base:

> The learning centers here at Williams AFB provide support to both the T-37 and T-38 phases of training through the audio/visual media. The two centers combined have a total of 47 student study carrels of which 5 are cockpit type, 8 for strictly study purposes, and the rest have sound on slide and/or super 8mm self contained equipment in them. From 53 super 8mm film programs and approximately 80 sound on slide programs just about every phase of flight and just about every emergency procedure that student pilots may encounter can be studied in detail on the ground in a relaxed atmosphere. Thus we are able to help reduce the psychological and physiological stress that always accompanies the task of piloting an aircraft.

Along with simulation, the uniqueness of the learning center is that student pilots may study virtually any task that's associated with piloting an aircraft on the ground under controlled conditions and then subsequently transferred to the sky. Inherent in this multi-media, self study, and student involvement, is achieved through "pause" features in just about all of our sound on slide programs. Another uniqueness is that words with pictures better fixes in the student pilots mind what various maneuvers look like. Consequently they can "dry fly" maneuvers on the ground.

Such armed services learning centers are developing for both training programs and for the educational programs provided for families of personnel. Such programs are not limited to U.S. installations but are also being developed in overseas dependent's schools.

The instructional development concept has become institutionalized within the armed services. Though it is not part of the learning center institution in the services, there is much to be learned from their developmental plan. An armed service branch might, for instance, need to train 500 new supply sergeants every six weeks. Under such a time constraint with large numbers of personnel going through the program, a good, highly defined program with as much individualization as possible is needed. Thus, through the ID process, the services are able to plan, utilize resources, and execute an institutional process which will maximize output and effect economies. It is surprising that with such success in the military establishment, educator, who on a national scale deal with far larger numbers of students, do not develop such highly defined courses!

In *industry and business* small learning center-like programs are being developed. While special libraries for information have always been important in the business and industrial sector, new forms of information-bearing media now are being used, and in-service personnel development is becoming very important. Independent studies for the executive needing to read faster, for the bank employee needing to learn a new routine, for the group needing to interact more effecitvely, etc. are becoming available. In the larger businesses and corporations learning centers can embrace more and more of the total LC concept. With diversified businesses and opportunities, the large corporation needs to guide its employees in upward and lateral career moves, to provide education for movement to new positions, and to provide the access to information for maintenance of present positions where one who does not continue to learn will soon be left behind, where the status quo does not exist but is a retrograding position.

Public libraries are unique institutions. Already funded and *there*, they are now beginning to offer many of the specialized services of learning centers. Some public libraries now offer videotaped mini-courses and undoubtedly many will soon begin to develop courses around their own resources. It is the author's firm conviction that unless the formal educational institutions accelerate their own offerings in diversified subject areas and in packaged formats, the public library may become a new wing of the educational establishment—a kind of public learning center, an educational laundromat which can be used at the time best suited to the individual. While such development of the public library is important, economics of funding will not be realized if too many "noneducational" institutions begin to drain resources from the educational institution.

Setting Up the Learning Center

The process of planning an LC calls for a commitment to introduce a number of functions new to the organization—functions which will initially face resistance from both within the LC and from the total institution. Thus, once an agreement has been made to integrate a number of learning functions, a series of programs can be used to involve students and faculty in the change process. These programs outlined below, while developing and implementing a general, predeveloped LC master plan, will also act to effect acceptance of the learning center concept within the total institution.

1. Involvement of faculty and students in all activities, in-

cluding initial planning. But even at initial stages, LC personnel should be ready to lead. Attention is centered on the learner and the learning process.

2. Development of the school's concept of the self-learner. By one definition the self-learner is one who is able to determine individual needs and to participate in the development of a program to meet those needs. For instance, one school may make use of its librarians in the development of the acquisition of information process and its counselors in the development of goal paths. The choice of such personnel for certain developmental tasks is determined as a function of the particular school's definition of the self-learner and of the school's available personnel resources.

3. Expansion of collections though a traditional concept. Exploration, evaluation, and acquisition provide learning experiences. Students as well as faculty are involved in this process.

4. Production and developmental activities defined. Once such definitions have been made, a whole range of unknown resources for such activity may be found either on campus or within the local community.

5. Learner and task analysis as concepts defined. Large amounts of time and money can be spent to determine learners strengths, weaknesses, and needs and to establish appropriate training tasks. But probably only through institutionalization of such activity can any appreciable change in education take place! The institution has to decide how serious it is, and to what degree it will commit resources to provide a program of individualized instruction.

6. Development of new learning environments. Though by far the easiest to conceptualize and the most "fun" at which to work, new learning environments are still difficult to develop. Educators and students must be brought to accept learning labs, gaming, mass informational devices such as computer, etc., and money must be located to support such activity.

7. Selective dissemination projects evolved to determine the informational needs of students and faculty and the ways to meet such needs.

8. Workshops set up for the improvement of learning through

behaviorally-oriented re-analysis of instructional technologies.

9. As a function of all of the above and as the program evolves, personnel to meet needs hired. Such personnel (discussed in detail in a later chapter) may well fall under several broad categories.

  a. Supply-Support function. This is the traditional function of any library of software and hardware and encompasses the basic selection, evaluation, acquisition, distribution/retrieval, description, and storage functions.

  b. Production function. When media is commercially unavailable, it must be provided. Personnel to generate new media (16-and 8-mm film, computer programs, video signals, etc.) and conventional media such as printed matter, slides, tapes, etc., must be trained or located.

  c. Instructional function. The learning center will provide a wide variety of instructional activities not tied to any other curriculum than its own. There may be activities such as training paraprofessionals, workshops to improve instruction, etc.

  d. Consultative function. Specialists will be needed to work with faculty and students in the selection, procurement, design, development, and execution of systematically designed stimulus material and environments.

  e. Administrative function. Someone with authority must be available to allocate resources, to tie program segments together, to stimulate evaluation, etc. Ideally such a person is a communicator, a public relations person, a hehavioral scientist, and a systems analyst.

Needs Assessment

One fundamental requirement for a genuinely useful learning center is a close working relationship with instructors. A learning center's variety of audiovisual equipment and instructional development services will amount to little if they are not used by the faculty. A "needs assessment" appears to be one logical way to find out what the services are that faculty would prefer.

It is recommended that a series of one-hour interviews with a substantial portion of the faculty (35 to 45 percent), be held to identify the instructional techniques which teachers feel have been effective in their classes, to obtain views on alternative instructional techniques, and to determine which media services are in use and what new types are desired in the future.

Responses to interview questions on the use of instructional techniques should yield a picture of faculty attitudes toard innovation in instruction. For example, consider the question:

It is commonly felt that the Instructional technique used in community colleges more often than any other is *lecturing*. Is this true for you in this course?

If the responses show 85 percent of faculty agreeing with the statement, the learning center staff will be required to lay a great deal of groundwork before much use of instructional development would occur. Instructors should also have ample opportunity to "dream" or brainstorm about the techniques they would use if they operated under no practical constraints. The result of this sort of questioning can be interesting: at times exciting ideas develop, on other occasions instructors who can't imagine any changes even under ideal conditions are exposed.

The area of evaluation should be examined. What types of tests does each instructor use and why? Are any other forms of feedback employed by faculty in addition to testing? The following question might provide necessary answers:

For certain kinds of learning and/or for certain people, it appears to be essential for learners to have sufficient opportunities (in addition to tests) to try out the competencies they are expected to achieve and to get information about results and corrections quickly. In this course:
a. Such feedback is provided.
b. Would be desirable but is not feasible.
c. Is not appropriate.

The actual current use of audiovisual hardware and services can be investigated by merely asking the instructor to list equipment used. It is important here to let the interviewee respond with little or no prompting, for often the instructor may say in an attempt to please the interviewer that almost all types of equipment are used.

If possible, the needs assessment should be done by an outside, impartial observer who has had some interviewing experience.

Once completed, needs assessment should provide first a profile of the faculty's attitudes on traditional or nontraditional instructional approaches and second, information concerning the level of current use of services.

A model for those wishing to utilize a needs assessment study upon which to base developmental decisions is provided in Appendix A.

Utilizing the LC Consultant

Not only is it best that the needs assessment be made by an outside, impartial observer as previously indicated, but in addition there is no doubt that the visiting expert or consultant can be quite valuable in setting up a learning center. Such an outside individual can bring new expertise, and, what is almost as important, can act as a sounding board for center personnel and the personnel in the school as a whole.

Several things can be done to optimize the visit of a consultant.

1. The school should provide very specific objectives for the consultant well before his visit. This will allow him to develop a specific "game plan," and he will not spend undue time trying to determine his role. Providing a "problem" is a very good idea.

2. If desired, the consultant may be used as a diffusion agent to communicate the major ideas of the learning center. Frequently, the consultant makes presentations to several campus groups.

3. The consultant should be given as much time as possible to meet with interested personnel. While the consultant may ask to speak to certain individuals, it is particularly important that he should be available to faculty who wish to raise questions or provide their own ideas.

4. The consultant must be given sufficient time to do the job —but not too much time. Consultative work is exhausing with much time spent in making presentations, talking to people,

visiting facilities and programs, etc. But the consultant will have come with a preconceived "set" on what a good center's operation should be like. It is that "set" which the school has purchased. The consultant will observe things as they are and will listen to people discuss how they would like things to be. Perhaps the most productive time will occur after the consultant has left the school. As the report is prepared, the consultant will bring years of experience and expertise to bear on a problem which has been defined by the school.

5. Don't expect too much from the consultant's visit. Long, overly worded reports may make the consultant's fee seem valuable, but a shorter report, directly to the subject is more easily used and far more likely to be read by the large audience to which it should be disseminated. The school should encourage the consultant to be frank and lucid.

6. Be fair to the consultant. A ten-hour day is fine, but only if prearranged and paid for. If a consultant is hired for three days and the report expected includes information (e.g., the school may expect very specific suggestions as to other consultants, equipment to purchase, places to contact for personnel, etc.) which will require several days search after leaving, pay for the total job in such a way that all time and expertise are recognized in the fee. A consultant from another school probably is not totally motivated by the fee, but if a reasonable fee is not paid a mediocre report may be received.

7. Finally, once the consultant has provided the report there must be carry through. The consultant can only suggest, the school must use or reject those suggestions in a planned way so that impetus will not be lost. Inertia is overcome when the decision to invite a consultant is made. Too often, once the report has been received, nothing else happens. The report will not be magic in itself. The people at the school must make that magic so that the learning center can be institutionalized.

The Learning Center Facilities

To ascertain proper space utilization, all present functions, plus those contemplated for the near future, and those contemplated for the distant future need to be considered for such characteristics as capacity, relationship to and mutuality with other functions, relative importance, traffic patterns, need for personnel, supervision, etc. The final facility configuration should be optimized for both the efficiency of the operation and its cost. Once learning center space needs have been stated, visits to other facilities should be undertaken. At this or a later time, consultant help may be utilized.

One of the most striking advantages of the learning center as an integrated, centralized resource is in space utilization. Better service with a decrease in space requirements will almost certainly be the product of integration. Most important, an optimum atmosphere for innovation, communication, program development, and learning improvement is provided by having functions and personnel of "various breeds" in close proximity.

A "Survey of Learning Center Facilities Requirements" is provided as Appendix B to help in determining space needs.

The Diffusion of Innovation

Acceptance of the idea of the learning center with its eventual activities depends upon a communication program which is open, persuasive, and directed to centers of innovation and power within the institution.

One of the major roles of the learning center is to be an agent for change. A vast social psychology literature exists upon which to base a program which accepts as its mandate activities leading to change in people and things. Using that literature, the information provided in figure XI attempts to map out a program established at De Anza College's Learning Center. A close study of the information in the figure will show that it is rich with ideas which may be redefined for another institution's change program.

As noted in the figure, initial work in a change program should begin with opinion leaders. These are the people to whom others look for ideas. Such leaders may be ready to adopt new ideas or may be resistant to change. The identification of opinion leaders should be easy, and once identified, they should be given the best service imaginable so that they can judge the program on its potential. In addition, opinion leaders should be given maximum information about all services and the extent of those

DIFFUSION AND ADOPTION OF LEARNING INNOVATION

Personnel to be Affected (with temporal priority ranking)	Activity to be Diffused and/or Adopted	Primary LC Faculty Diffusion Activities
OPINION LEADERS	Instructional Development	A, H
	LC Utilization	A, F, G, H
	Media Evaluation and Acquisition	D, G
INTERESTED FACULTY	Instructional Development	H
	LC Utilization	E
	Media Evaluation and Acquisition	D, G
DIVISION HEADS	Encourage Non-traditional Approaches to Learning	E, F
	Encourage LC Utilization	A, F
COLLEGE ADMINISTRATION	Support LC Activity with Monies and Opportunity	A, D, H
TEACHING FACULTY	Instructional Development	A, E, F, H
	LC Utilization	A, C, G, H
	Media Evaluation and Acquisition	A, G
STUDENTS	LC Utilization	A, G, H, J
	Acceptance of Non-traditional Learning Environments	B, D, G
DISTRICT ADMINISTRATION	Support LC Activity with Monies and Opportunity	A, B, H
GOVERNING BOARD	Support LC Activity by Policy	B, D, G

DIFFUSION ACTIVITIES

A -personal contact	F -departmental meetings
B -small group meeting	G-literature dissemination
C-large group meeting	H-service
D-Demonstration projects	I -mandate change
E -Workshops	J -Classes

Figure XI

services provided by the learning center. Whenever possible a low profile should be maintained in this communication program so as not to accentuate what to many will already look like an attempt to replace many of the functions of the classroom.

In establishing a learning center, LC personnel work with people who still are used to the customary model of education—the classroom. Educators are so often pressed by the necessity of preparing for the next class lesson that they do not feel that they have the luxury to even consider innovation, let alone work on it. The learning center personnel must take the initiative to assure their teachers and administrators are given sufficient time to consider innovations. Then LC personnel must optimize the use of that time, make the ouput very demonstrable, and reduce the threat of innovation—approaching the changes as positive, attainable, and desirable.

Setting up the learning center is a complex operation. It is more than a change in names, facilities, and resources. It is foremost a change in attitude and in the reallocation of resources.

IV

Learning Center Specialists

With the immense diversification of services provided within
a learning center, it is not surprising that personnel talent must
be drawn from varied fields and that as the center grows and
responsibility increases, that talent must become more specialized—with greater depth of expertise. This need for the specialist is one which may be resisted by many of the tradition-ori-
ented people who worked in the library or media center before it
became a learning center. The resistance to specialization—
which in essence is support for the generalist—is based on days
when personnel in college were given training courses of a
general nature which prepared them to be "all things to all
people." Although the librarian could perform various functions
including reference, cataloging media, circulation of books,
administration etc., the audiovisualist could circulate hardware
and software, evaluate and utilize media, produce software, etc.,
and the learning handicapped specialist could diagnose all
problems, prescribe new activities, counsel, etc., there is need
for trained specialists for a truly effective learning center. Who
are they, and where can they be located? (The use of paraprofessionals and their roles must be a function of the particular
center's resources and priorities, so the paraprofessional is not
considered in this book.)

As the center becomes larger and more and more a focusing point for an instrumentation of change in the school, the center's personnel must become more specialized and more capable of making dramatic moves. They must be on, or create, the cutting edge of new thinking. More than likely (and to the center's advantage) this specialization will be built upon a broad generalist-based training program. Without such a general educational foundation, the commonality of experience and purpose will be missing and the movement of the specialist into a central location in the mainstream will be most difficult. The instructor working with an instructional development specialist who has never taught is unlikely to be led. On the other hand, with a background of teaching kinship, teamwork can be developed leading to an improved educational product.

Personnel Functions

Supply-Support Function
The traditional function of any library of materials, encompasses the basic selection, evaluation, and distribution/retrieval routines with the attendant customary tasks of description and storage. Almost all media, print or nonprint, except for some electronic data forms such as computer generations, lend themselves to the library-like routines and tasks taught in library science curricula. Personnel for such functions should be readily available from library science programs and are probably already available in most centers.

Production Function
A newer function for the center, production suggests a wide variety of activities from providing descriptive booklists and leaflets on how to use the center to the generation of new media such as 16-and 8-mm films, slides, video programs, computer programs, and total learning packages. New specialists trained in a number of communication skills are needed for such activities and should be readily available from audio visual, television, and instructional technology training programs.

Academic (Instructional) Function

The instructional function of the learning center is one which, though recognized, has seldom been formalized. It suggests a wide variety of activities on an informal to formal continuum. There are such informal activities as having the specialist visit the classroom to teach center utilization or to conduct usage tours of the center. At a halfway point there are such quasi-formal activities as in-service workshops for faculty or for local district personnel in the utilization of media. On a formal level there is the development of a number of training programs for media paraprofessionals. As taboos with regard to graduate credit are broken down, professional graduate education, especially for in-service staff development, may well also find its place in the learning center. The professional capable of functioning in this way already may be available in most centers.

Consultative (Development) Function

As the most innovative function of the center, the consultative function requires a new specialist or the retrained generalist. Such a specialist should be available to work with faculty and students in the selection, procurement, development, and execution of systematically designed stimulus material. In such a role, the specialist may provide help in developing an auto-tutorial lab for a botany class, may work with a student in designing a class presentation, may work on individual learning problems, or may work to develop various types of stimulus materials. As long as training programs view media functions merely as support functions on the periphery of instruction such specialists will be difficult to find.

Administrative Function

Program identity, policy, direction, and cohesion can best be coordinates through the administrator of the center who developmentally allocates resources. Practically, it will be difficult to find the individual described here (more than likely, the administrator must be developed), but logically a generalist in both print and nonprint media systems with specialization in administration is needed. To also provide for innovative development, in addition there must be understanding of the broad principles of systems development and the potentials for diffusion and adoption activity.

Other Functions

Many other functions will occur as a result of the center's broad service paradigm. Specialists will have to be located who understand the psychology of the special learner, who understand the function of the tutorial and independent modes of learning, etc. There will be programs to provide training for some (such as the specialist who works with the educationally handicapped) and there will be some specialists (such as tutorial) who may of necessity gain expertise on the job.

Most of these functions are highly interrelated and do not necessarily indicate that different specialists are needed for each. Furthermore, there could be additional specialists. In larger centers, for instance, different production specialists might well be available for audio/video, motion picture and still photography, graphics, computer program design, etc. The functions, described above, do indicate that for a center to provide an innovative climate, a variety of human resources should be available. The educator from outside the center can then make use of any or all of the center's resources desired, whether traditional print, nonprint, the physical environment alone, personnel alone, or any combination.

Personnel Specialists

In the past, the non-human resources for a learning center have been stressed. Technology is an extension of man which requires man; administrators must strive to supply this most important resource. As the learning center concept is enlarged, innovative practices with far-reaching goals may well provide totally different learning environments and practices. New practices will require specialists as yet neither identified nor available.

A few position descriptions are given and discussed below to provide examples for those developing learning center needs.

The Learning Disabilities Specialist

(adapted from a description by Judy Triana, De Anza College)

The Learning Disabilities Specialist must be trained in the area of special education or related fields and needs the diagnostic skills necessary to determine the appropriate direction of a student's program of learning. Such a specialist works as part of a team, and brings to the program a particular knowledge of an area of instruction (i.e., reading, language, educational psychology or counseling) in addition to general diagnostic skills.

The Specialist's role is to plan and effect the diagnostic evaluations and prescriptive instructional programs for each of the students in the class.

Specific responsibilities are:

1. Diagnostic—testing and observation
   a. To administer normed and/or functional tests of language, perception, memory, input and output skills; and a general achievement test of performance in basic subject areas.
   b. To interpret the results and suggest developmental or remedial approaches specially suited to the individual student.
   c. To observe the student's performance in learning situations throughout the quarter and share this information with instructional and counseling personnel.
   d. To obtain information relevant to the student's learning problem from medical, psychological, educational and social sources.

2. Educational—perscriptive teaching
   a. To design and supervise the development of instructional material specially suited to the student and guide him to available materials on campus.
   b. To supervise the tutors assigned to his students in direct cooperation with the Tutorial Center staff.
   c. To consult with subject-matter instructors regarding specific students and materials.
   d. To act as a learning specialist as part of the instructional development team.

The Chief Administrator of the Center

(adapted from a description by George Voegel, Dean of Learning Resources, William Rainey Harper Community College)

The title used for the chief administrator of the center varies greatly from place to place, but for the purpose of this description let us use "dean."

The dean of learning resources is directly responsible to the vice-president of academic affairs for the development and effective operation of the Learning Resources Center. The dean will also serve as a staff officer to the vice-president for other duties and responsibilities as prescribed for this position.

The Dean of Learning Resources:

1. Assists the vice-president of academic affairs, together with other deans, in planning and organizing the educational programs of the college and plans and implements the LRC programs and services to support these educational programs.
2. Assists the vice-president and other staff with instructional development and innovative instruction.
3. Develops and implements procedures and processes designed to increase student and staff use of LRC services and facilities.
4. Assists the vice-president with planning, development and implementation of faculty orientation.
5. Plans, develops, and implements a faculty LRC in-service program.
6. Develops and recommends requirements and qualifications for new LRC staff.
7. Evaluates and make recommendations in regards to selection, promotion, leaves, and retention, non-retention, and tenure of all LRC staff and maintain appropriate records.
8. Provides input into recommendations regarding retention, non-retention, promotion, and tenure appointments of full-time teaching faculty.
9. Provides appropriate input to division chairmen in writing objectives for LRC and performance appraisals based on these objectives.
10. Provides for effective and efficient support to the instruc-

tional programs and other college services through the appropriate directors of resources, processing, and production services for the on-going LRC functions of circulation, reference, systems design and maintenance, acquisition and cataloging, and TV and graphic production of learning materials.

11. Plans, develops, and recommends to the vice-president the LRC annual budget and administers the adopted budget.
12. Evaluates the LRC operations and services and make recommendations for improvement of these services to the college staff and students and to the community.
13. Prepares and/or makes other studies on LRC services as requested by president or vice-president.
14. Coordinates and encourages participation in professional development for all LRC staff.
15. Assists vice-president in coordinating liaison activities with state agencies, community groups, other community colleges, four-year colleges and universities in regards to LRC services.

While such a job description is tied to the specific point-of-view and the needs of the authoring college, it is evident that the chief administrator is indeed an administrator with knowledge of all aspects of the center and with particular administrative talents in such areas as evaluation budget, resource allocation, systems, and diffusion of ideas.

Instructional Development Specialist

The following description adapted from the one developed by the author for the specialist at De Anza College points up a particular situation which will be evident in many developing centers. While the specialist has a particular, very definite job to do (in this case as an instructional developer), in addition there may be dual responsibilities (in this case supervising the audiovisual program). Such dual responsibilities are frequently required since to date both availability of trained personnel and budget needs often prohibit having different specialists for each function.

Working with personnel in the Learning Center, the instructional development specialist:

1. Supervises an audiovisual services program.
2. Supervises a local production program.
3. Acts as team leader in the instructional development process to aid the individual faculty member in solving educational problems, developing mini courses and micro-units, creating courses, or redeveloping old ones through a process calling for
   a. analysis of learning tasks,
   b. analysis of audience characteristics,
   c. specification of desirable learning goals and behavioral objectives,
   d. selection and design of appropriate strategies and learning environments,
   e. selection, acquisition, production and evaluation of instructional media.
4. Acts as a consultant to individual faculty members on individualizing and/or programing learning experience, hardware and software resources, and media systems such as television, audio retrieval, etc.

Professional qualifications for the ID specialist include a valid credential entitling the individual to hold a certified faculty position; a minimum of a Master's degree (or equivalent experience) in instructional technology, and a knowledge of learning theory and practical teaching experience.

Personal qualifications needed are sensitivity to the values, goals, and needs of community college faculty and students; ability to work and communicate openly with faculty and students on a one-to-one basis and in a group mode; an openness and responsiveness to innovative learning approaches, and knowledge of and ability to work with minority groups and women and other representatives of a diverse population on the campus and in the community.

The point regarding working on a one-to-one basis with the faculty and students can not be overstressed. The specialist must be capable and sure of himself and in this assuredness willing to see himself wholly as only the facilitator of projects. Though not self-demeaning, this specialist must be willing to acknowledge that the instructor, for instance, is the "boss," that the instructor is to be served.

Equally important, the developer should work toward eliminating his job. While "everything" may be done for a few instructor, the developer will not be able to significantly affect a total school's educational program unless he works with many people. Thus, the specialist must during the process of developing a particular instructional unit, give the instructor skills so that future development can be handled by that instructor. The developer must cultivate the instructor's skills until that instructor can function alone, only calling on those paraprofessional skills which it would be inefficient to provide for himself.

Staff Development Specialist

The following description extracted from the job description by the author for the specialist at De Anza College is interesting in that it points up how such a description can really be a list of expected outcomes from the specialist.

Examples of Duties: Working with all segments, full and part-time, of the college staff (certificated and classified), the staff development specialist develops a comprehensive program of developmental activities.

1. Organizes and develops a variety of activities for the total staff in such areas on inservice education, travel, conferences, etc.
2. With the instructional development specialist develops inservice experiences in techniques of instruction, utilization of media, testing, instructional development as a process, learning theory, etc.
3. With the Dean of Instruction for Personnel institutes a program which encourages staff members to establish individualized, personal development plans.
4. With the Dean of Student Services originates a program which makes personal counseling, communications skills and ethnic/cultural awareness inservice education, and personnel service consultation available to all staff.
5. With the head librarian, locate, review, and disseminate appropriate research findings, methodologies, and educational innovations which may be important to the staff.
6. Develops a comprehensive reassigned time plan for the total college which accounts for already available resources

such as sabbaticals, research and innovation funds, administrative funds, etc. and which adds additional resources as needed.

7. Develops a recognition system for staff for a variety of of performances.
8. Develops and directs an internship program for the staff.
9. Disseminates any appropriate activities (as outlined previously) to other staffs such as those of local elementary and secondary schools and training programs in local business and industry.
10. Teaches appropriate inservice classes.

Finding the Specialist

In most cases the movement toward creating a center is based upon the utilization of present resources and most people currently employed will neither quit, die, nor be fired from the institution. Rather, they must be utilized in new roles with new expectations. Thus a large part of the creation of the center from an already available base will be in redeveloping personnel. A strong program of in-service, continuing education, and redeployment of personnel must take place.

For a totally new center, there is the unique opportunity and responsibility to select new personnel to function in the roles the center's conceptual architects will have specified.

Although looking for new personnel is easier than developing the old, it is not necessarily an easy task. For instance, over seventy-five graduate programs exist in the United States for the development of personnel described by these programs as persons able to function as media specialists, instructional developers, audiovisualists, instructional technologists, and in a number of other such job titles. But the quality and actual expertise of people from different programs under even the exact same title varies greatly. Thus, since there are no standards for specialist training programs (at least there are accredited programs for librarians—as suspect as that accreditation criterial process is, the school developing a new learning center must be able to specify its exact needs and be able to scrutinize candidates closely to obtain the best person to meet the particular school's needs.

For the academic media school, the supply-demand question for media personnel in the future will be answered by a combination of interacting factors. Media schools themselves will have the opportunity to improve their own potential if they can assess the factors which will determine the types and numbers of media personnel which will be needed in coming years. With a sagging economy and a pitiful lack of good research data, the identification of future media specializations and the need for them are somewhat conjectural at this point. However, it is highly likely that some differentiated staffing models will appear in the next few years which should indicate some guidelines for planning. Certainly, it seems that instructional development will be a major area for future specialization—especially if a technology for learning and several good developmental models can be presented.

Indiana University's Division of Instructional Systems Technology has, for instance, masters, two-year graduate, and doctoral programs in instructional media and technology. Within each of these degrees there are a wide number of options and specializations. In their doctoral and two-year graduate degree programs there are six curricular areas which can be emphasized: instructional television, instructional design and development, product evaluation and curricular integration, systems design and management of learning resource programs, message design and production, and diffusion and adoption of innovations in instructional systems technology. Furthermore, students are encouraged to achieve special competencies in such areas as computer technology, educational media in areas of rapid change, programmed instruction, and writing for educational media.

Again, because of the wide variance of training programs such as the large one at Indiana with multiple courses and various specialty areas and those which are less well-defined and with fewer options, it is imperative that the center administrator have clear criteria for the new jobs, as well as be aware of the schools producing such personnel, and furthermore that

87

the administrator provide as wide a distribution of job descriptions as possible.

In order to specify criteria as meaningfully as possible to best make use of present personnel or select new ones, the information in figure XII is provided. By expanding such a chart both vertically to consider other competencies and horizontally to consider other areas of training, the administrator can arrive at decisions on personnel utilization more systematically.

LEARNING CENTER
RESPONSIBILITY FLOW DETERMINANTS

	SPECIALISTS	
	TRAINING IN PRINT AREAS	TRAINING IN NON-PRINT AREAS
Acquisitions		
1. Selection	XX	XX
2. Evaluation	XX	XX
3. Ordering	XX	
Technical Handling		
1. Cataloging	XX	
2. Processing	XX	
Distribution		
1. Hardware		XX
2. Software	XX	
Production		XX
Allocation of Human Resources (Administration)	?	?
Allocation of Non-Human Resources (Administration)	XX	XX
Learning: Developmental Activity in Area of Instruction		XX
Learning: Developmental Activity in Area of Non-traditional Learning Environments	XX	XX
Learning: Supportive Collection Maintenance	XX	
Utilization Workshops		
1. Print	XX	
2. Non-Print		XX
Learning Center Utilization Orientation	XX	XX
Diffusion and Adoption Activity (probably most important function)	XX	XX

Figure XII

Allocating Specialist Time

The model in figure XIII is useful in allocating personnel time. Once system needs are determined and those needs are expressed in terms of time, it is possible to assign personnel to meet those needs. In assigning such personnel time, both expertise and interest must be considered. If only one person with the needed expertise is available, the allocation is easy, but if

DE ANZA COLLEGE LEARNING CENTER
FACULTY AND STAFF REALLOCATION, 1972-73

SYSTEM* NEEDS (in priority ranking)	NEEDS EXPRESSED IN HOURS REQUIRED PER WEEK	PERSONNEL AVAILABLE WITH NEEDED EXPERTISE	PERSONNEL INTEREST?	PERSONNEL ALLOCATION
2. Circulation	110	Classified (100) J. R. (10)	Yes	Classified (100) J. R. (10)
3. Diffusion activity promoting LC utilization	20	No one	Everyone	Informal basis (10)** G. P. (10)
5. Media (print) evaluation and selection	LC Print Faculty (20) DAC Faculty (?)	All LC Faculty DAC Faculty	Yes	LC Faculty (20) DAC Faculty as needed
6. Media (non-print) evaluation selection	5	W. S.	Yes	W. S. (5)
7. Selection and acquisition coordination (5 and 6)	40 classified 10 certificated	J. H. E. M.	Yes	J. H. (40) E. M. (10)
8. Graphics	50 +	M. J. (40)	Yes	M. J. (40)
10. Reference	68	a. V. O (37½) b. G. K. (20) c. Others (10½)	a. Yes b. Yes c. ?	V. O. (30) G. K. (15) Others (23)
15. Coordinated Learning Lab	20	J. R. (10) W. S. (10)	Yes	J. R. (10) W. S. (5)
39. Innovation Time	32	Everyone	Yes	Everyone, 4 hours per week
TOTALS	(X)	(Y)		(X? Y?) (Z) (Y? X?)

*Does not, but could, include students.
**At times not assigned, such as lunch, does not count in number of hours available.
 Z is diminished by committee work, meetings, sickness, etc.

Figure XIII

several are available, then the best person with an interest in the task should be assigned.

By ranking the LC system's needs on a priority basis, it is easy to identify new personnel needs and to determine which system needs can not be met because of lack of personnel. If such a model for personnel allocation or reallocation is not adopted, then efficiency will be difficult to maintain and more than likely, high priority tasks will not be completed due to the utilization of resources on lower priority ones. (A second staffing model developed by Mary Jensen, Director of Learning Resources, West Valley College, Saratoga, California, is provided as Appendix C.)

As school populations decrease, the utilization of the total school's work force must be reconsidered. The present dwindling of school populations suggests the opportunity to move from traditional learning environments to less traditional ones. With such a move and the possibility that the impetus of such a move may occur in the learning center, the opportunity to make use of teaching faculty no longer needed in the classroom in new roles in the center is a real possibility. Such a reallocation provides new resources for program development and again sug-

INSERT FIG. XIV ABOUT HERE

gests the need for in-service and continuing education so that new specializations can be developed.

To summarize then, the greatest resource of and potential for the learning center is its personnel. In a rapidly changing educational milieu, new roles must be assumed and these roles require greater substance and depth than ever before. Specialization is the only way to provide these roles. But specialization should be based on a solid, generalist education so that personnel are able to communicate with the many users of the center and so that a unified, educationally sound center can be developed.

LEARNING CENTER SPECIALISTS

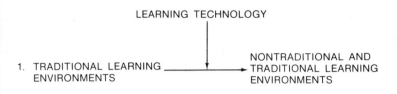

1. TRADITIONAL LEARNING ENVIRONMENTS ⟶ NONTRADITIONAL AND TRADITIONAL LEARNING ENVIRONMENTS

LEARNING TECHNOLOGY

2. EMERGENCE OF DIFFERENTIATED EDUCATIONAL ROLES.

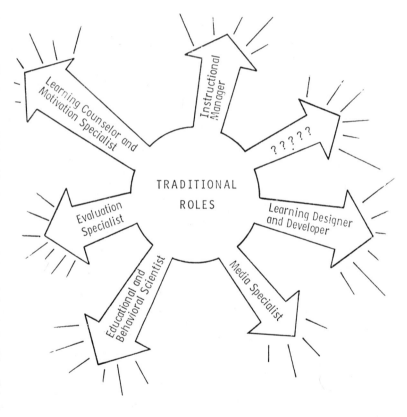

Figure XIV

V

The Center and Change

The major activity upon which the learning center is based is CHANGE. Our consideration of this change is fourfold: a general consideration of the management of change; academic program change through personnel development; the instructional development suite as a vehicle for change; and internal change through a specific management program.

The Management of Change

That change should be a peculiar progeny of the learning center should not be surprising. Concerned with both instruction and student needs, the center is in the unusual position of having to do what other areas may only espouse. The student personnel service, for instance, is typically not competent to help students whose difficulties are almost totally academic. Then, too, the divisional head, departmental dean, dean of instruction, or other administrative leader is too often tied to the minutiae of a day-to-day job. These instructional leaders are often "under-read" and hence ill informed on new practices, overly protective of the faculties they have hired, and inclined to promote only traditional practices. The center, then, with its unique competencies and roles is likely to fall heir to promoting useful change on campus, and such a change in role may well become the major activity of the center.

Like the agriculture extension service which provided the newest information to farmers and like the experimental farms which generated this new information, the learning center has several roles including not only the dissemination of new information but also the development of specialized information. Through its library of information the LC can provide the latest instructional technique and subject area development to the instructor. Through use of a selective dissemination of information project within the LC, the harried instructor can obtain succinct, vital information upon which to make decisions on instructional strategies and subject area considerations.

The generation of new techniques or information is also a role of the LC. The learning center should provide space and support to instructors for experimentation with new techniques. Within the LC the search is important and failure (nonsuccess) can be an appropriate outcome of any experiment. Space should be available, for instance, so that an instructor who wants to try a new technique (such as an auto-tutorial approach) may "lease" the space for a semester. For all who wish to plan and manage change in education, the learning center should be given the role of providing the opportunity for change and that role should be widely and explicitly promoted. By institutionalizing the process for change, by clearly pointout out where its resources are administered, what those resources are, and how they can be utilized, change as a natural, growth inducing, self-renewing process will be more easily managed.

If change is natural to life, and if educators are to control that change rather than being pushed along by it, then clear future goals must be provided. Though the learning center may provide information as to what is happening at other schools, as to what futurists are predicting, as to what new ideas are emerging, the total school staff must come together to provide the school's goal formation. One of the roles the center can have is sparking the generation of goals which will provide the parameter for change. Once such goals are spelled out, the learning center will be able to provide resources so that change is not overpowering for the individual.

Personnel Development

Since change occurs around us so rapidly and since educators believe in a nonstatic approach to learning, it is as important to provide opportunities for development and personal improvement for the faculty and staff of the school as it is to provide such opportunities for students; a mature, developed personnel will be far more capable of directing the development of the student's potentials.

The elements of a personnel development program are many, including such things as in-service study, personal counseling, travel, retreats, the availability of resources and information about trends and new ideas, etc. But even more important, a comprehensive program which deals with all of a school's working staff (teaching, administrative, counseling, LC, clerical, custodial, etc.) must be provided to bring all staff together so that they may have an opportunity to know each other and so that goals may be generated from the broadest possible base, and so that a community feeling may be developed.

The learning center can have several roles in such a program: administration of the program, provision of in-service workshops, space, etc. Learning center resources such as the professional library and instructional development can greatly aid a general personnel development program.

But a personnel development program's greatest resource is its own personnel. If personnel can be directed and used to help each other, the program is likely to be a success. The learning center can help provide for such personnel utilization in a number of ways. Besides redeploying teaching faculty into nonteaching roles within the center on a permanent basis, temporary redeployment is possible. The following project developed by the author is based on the teaching faculty member's need for *time*, time which can be used for change. The project may provide a useful model for others wishing to experiment with redeploying faculty.

Faculty Development Grants for Instructional Change.
Purpose: to examine, develop and evaluate new designs for classroom instruction.
Costs: salaries for two teachers for one quarter and $2000 for supplies.
Plan:

Phase I (Spring Quarter)
On the basis of submitted plans, two grants will be provided through the Office of Instruction to instructors
1. who are to be released from all teaching responsibilities for the quarter.
2. to work forty hours per week in the development of new designs for instruction.
3. to conduct such projects in the Learning Center environment.
4. to design or redesign a presently offered class (es) (large or small) which they are teaching.
5. to examine and develop an instructional sequence supported by written objectives, strategies, developed media, evaluations instruments, etc.

Phase II (Summer)
During the summer session, each grantee will present an instructional development workshop to other faculty members and selected local educators in the related discipline. Emphasis shall be placed on (1) the team approach and process of instructional development, (2) a demonstration of course repackaging and experimental strategies, etc., (3) the necessity for output and evaluation, (4) in any one workshop, student will be from the same general discipline as the teacher—providing for a common ground for strategy consideration.

Phase III (Fall Quarter)
Each grantee will implement his newly designed approach to instruction.

Phase IV (Winter Quarter)
Each grantee will report the results of his project. The reports will be prepared for publication for De Anza College faculty and for sharing with other community colleges.

Note: Grantees will be assisted by the Office of Research in designing, updating and validating of research.

Such a project has many benefits. It tests the idea of time being a major barrier to change, provides for improved instruction, allows the instructor to gain new competencies, causes the instructor to pass on competencies to fellow instructors, reports back vital information to the total faculty, and diffuses the concept of instructional development. The whole program on a continuing basis creates a stable atmosphere of sharing between professionals. Also it creates many instructional developers who are improving their own instruction as well as helping their peers develop better instruction, thus diffusing the skills of instructional development.

Instructional Development Suite

Within the learning center the instructional development suite as a complex of rooms for a variety of developmental activities has great potential for facilitating change. A discussion of the various rooms or areas should indicate how the program can be developed.

Facilitation Area.
When an instructor has made the decision to seek aid from instructional development, the initial contact should be as positive, goal-oriented, and directive as possible. Needs should be ascertained, meetings set up, and expectancies listed. Before leaving, the instructor should know when the next meeting will be and what can be expected from it. The facilitation process is really a filter which pre-screens, determines needs, bolsters egos, and outlines to the client what will be available through the ID service.

Design Area.

Here is where the important decisions are made. In a pleasant atmosphere, the teacher works with a team. Once the initial meeting (at which the team meets, the project is outlined, and the teacher is informed what his and other's roles are) is completed, the instructor will begin to design instruction, meet with team members when help is needed and occasionally meet with the whole team to assess progress and to keep everyone up-to-date on the project.

Production Area.

As its name indicates, this is the area where the nonprint media, graphics, booklets, handouts, etc. are actually produced. The area might have specialists in film, graphics, writing, printings computer programing, etc. The area should be close to the design area so consultation between designers and producers will be facilitated.

Implementation Area.

Before strategies can properly be tried in the classroom or other learning areas, testing should occur. The learning center may be able to provide an implementation area such as a model classroom with all of the paraphenalia of modern educational technology. In such an atmosphere and with the help of selected students, the instructor can evaluate the instruction, updating it until it meets specified criterial levels. Furthermore, having a model classroom may provide the instructor with ideas and an impetus for developing his own classroom into a more useful learning environment.

The implementation area can also be used as the prime classroom area for inservice workshops. Such scheduled workshops will thus be offered in an optimum learning environment and will provide a way to get personnel to come into the learning center.

This instructional development suite and its service specialists can provide a powerful process center to facilitate change. Good facilities do promote change!

Internal Change Management Program

If the growing edge of the specialist and that of the organization are to coincide, to stretch out (indeed, if they are to be
congruent enough to implement the short and long term plans
for the learning center) then a highly visible, personalized, and
easily utilizable plan for individuals must be sculptured. A
management by objective system, the MBO, can provide a
mechanism for orderly, planned change. It is positive, provides
individual and group feedback on and for development, and,
as written behavioral objectives provide a verbal type of "truth
in learning," the MBO puts "everything up front" so that there
is no question where priorities exist and where people hope to go.

Objectives provide for evaluation based on production. The
products should be from new, developmental tasks which may
be emphasized during a particular time frame so that they may
be completed during the time or tried out to test their efficacy
with regard to institutional needs.

Such objectives usually have three elements: (1) what is to be
accomplished; (2) under what conditions accomplishment will
occur (conditions are often understood and need not be stated);
(3) what are the criteria for success completion. In order to
facilitate the use of MBOs in the learning center, a simple plan
is presented here.

Step one: the learning center administrator meets with the
specialist. At this meeting each discusses his vision of the center's needs and how the specialists interests and competencies
may relate to those needs.

Step two: the specialist submits a list of MBO statements to
the administrator.

Step three: the administrator and the specialist again meet
to agree on objectives and formalize the plan including a statement of all conditions of it.

Step four: all sets of objectives are published so that everyone is "put on record" and so that input and help from others
can be expedited.

Step five: The administrator and specialist meet on a regular
basis to consider progress, to determine continuing appropriateness of objectives (they may be modified or eliminated when

necessary and by mutual agreement), and to eliminate or bypass, if possible, anything which has created blockage to goal success.

Step six: at the end of the period specified for activities (usually a school year) the administrator and specialist meet to discuss the period's activities, evaluate goal attainment, and to begin to plan the following period's goal plan.

Through careful management of time, the planning process just described should require minimal time so that time will be invested in the actual objectives. Most important, the plan will provide a way for individual specialists to develop personally and professionally and to support the mission of the school.

Several examples of objective statements are provided in Appendix D.

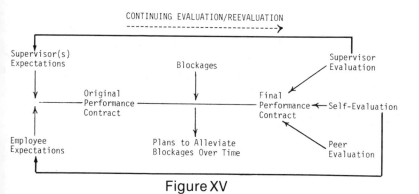

Figure XV

VI

State of the Art

It seems appropriate that having started with considerations of the concepts for a learning center, and discussed how the LC could be developed, we should end with a look at how centers exist today and how they might be evaluated. This actualization of the concept as exemplified by a variety of very different centers should finally indicate how very versatile the concept is and how it can be customized to meet the school's individual needs.

CAEMAT Study

Through a grant from the California Association for Educational Media and Technology the author in 1974 completed a study of the learning center in U.S. community colleges. The community college was chosen as the experimental population since the author was most familiar with the center at this level and since the literature indicated that the learning center was evolving most rapidly in the community college.

During late 1973 and early 1974, questionnaire responses were received from over 300 of the community colleges (all 950 public colleges were queried) in the U.S. The questionnaire

100

was designed to relate the concepts of a library of materials which is supportive of education and accomodates the self-contained classroom-teacher model and the newer concepts such as instructional development activities which initiate a more scientific, systematic approach to the improvement and individualization of learning experiences. These concepts and the provision of audiovisual services and a variety of nontraditional learning activities which completed the LC model were studied in order to verify or reject the author's conceptual model.

Findings

1. While the four-part model of library and AV services, instructional development, and nontraditional services and activities was a hyptotetical one before the research, 46.7 percent of the respondents indicated that their center did indeed contain all four components of the model. This verified the model's existence in reality.

2. In centers containing all the components, over 60 percent had these components located in one building. In the early developmental stage of the LC concept this centralization is not surprising. It is probable that the historical evolution of this total service grew within the building known as the library. The author would hypotehsize that as the concept and its actualization continue to grow and strengthen, facilities outside one building will of necessity be sought—both for space and to provide certain services closer to the patron.

3. When the model was not completely actualized with all four components, most learning resource centers (generically) provided library and AV services with almost 63 percent also having some nontraditional types of learning spaces or services. Instructional development services only existed in 16.7 percent of these centers and were fully absent from 82.1 percent of the schools. Thus, if instructional development was not provided by the learning center, the service probably did not exist at all on the campus.

4. More of the centers called themselves "Learning Resource Center" than "Library." To be exact, 38.4 percent called themselves a "Learning Resource Center," 29.2 percent called themselves a "Library," 7.5 percent called themselves a "Library/

Learning Resource Center," 3.3 percent call themselves a "Learning Center," and 21.7 percent used some other title. While this rejects the author's particular favorite title, the importance of the figures cannot be overemphasized. The rejection of the older, loved rubric "Library" in search of a new title indicates that movement is ocurring in schools, that there had been an acceptance of the new and the innovative.

5. Even though 142 schools had all four LC components and 29 more had instructional development, only 59 had a full-time development specialist. The commitment of personnel to a program is one of the best indicators of both its status and its future. Surely then, instructional development with all its potential is the weak area of service in most centers.

6. The nonpersonnel resources of centers are highly varied. More and more such unexpected media services as printing, sophisticated media production such as 16-mm film, and open and closed circuit television are becoming the expected. Furthermore, tutorial, skills and reading labs, computer and independent studies, and learning disabilities programs and rounding out facilities as they become true learning centers.

For a fuller report on the study, readers should contact either CAEMAT or the author.

Learning Centers

Several interesting reports from the field are presented here, for they not only contain information but point up differences. What various centers emphasize is a result of their individually perceived needs, and what the LC concept has given them is the flexibility to meet those needs in direct and exciting ways.

Oklahoma Christian College.

(Letter to the author from Bailey B. McBride, Associate Dean of the College)

"In response to your recent letter concerning the Mabee Learning Center and its operation, the central feature is a dial access system which provides for 132 different channels (that is, the system allows us to play 132 different tapes at one time) and 1,000 individual study carrels. When the Learning Center was constructed, the College provided a carrel for each student. Since then we have grown about 20 percent and although we still provide all students a carrel, not all have dial positions. Our experience has taught us that dial access is most useful for classes having a fairly large enrollment; consequently, we have made the most use of learning center materials with our general education program.

"At the beginning, we tried some unusual scheduling patterns which would reduce the number of class meetings for a certain course and then provided audiotaped instruction. Subsequently we have gone back to a more traditional patterning, and teachers often use audiotaped material in the same way that they would use reference or reserve books in the library. The principal difference is that almost all of the materials which are used through the learning center system are prepared by our own professors.

"In the summer we normally have a system of stipends so that faculty members can have time to work on materials for their courses. Not all the materials utilize audiotape instruction, but that technique has prompted faculty members to be much more innovative and creative in finding ways to help students learn.

"The learning center and library are under my supervision, and we conduct business by assigning each full-time employee a special duty and then every two weeks meet to resolve any problems of policy or operations. In the learning center we have three full-time employees, a director of audiovisual services, a director of dial access facilities, and a general engineer who oversees maintenance and keeps abreast of our current equipment status and needs. The library budget is approximately $80,000 per year, and the budget for learning center operations is approximately $70,000 excluding building maintenance and maintenance on the carrels themselves. Actually we have spent less on maintenance than we will have to at a later time since most of our equipment is relatively new and requires a minimum of maintenance."

Cuesta College.
(Letter to the author from Lyn Vivrette, Head Librarian).

103

"The Learning Center at Cuesta College is a two-story building located in the center of the campus. The Center contains all the traditional library services and collections (all multimedia materials are fully cataloged and integrated into the collection without regard to format), along with a self-study center, a tutorial center, an individualized video self-tutorial center, a career planning and counseling center, and several group instruction areas fully integrated on the main floor of the Learning Center. The audiovisual support center (campus distribution, production, etc.) and the audio-tutorial laboratories occupy part of the ground floor. The administration, counseling, guidance, and student services are temporarily located on the lower floor within demountable walled areas, to allow for future expansion of the Learning Center. The Learning Center is connected to every classroom, laboratory and facility on campus by a huge multiplicity of conduits for distribution of computer, video, audio and future programs, and is designed to interface with the commercial television cable services in order to bring programs into the community's individual homes.

"The uniqueness of the Cuesta Learning Center begins with outstanding team planning (including *professional* Learning Center planners and consultants) and a challenging philosophy: " 'The Learning Center is to meet the *individual* and *changing* needs of each student and *individual* and *changing* needs of each instructor . . . now and in the future.'

"To support this philosophy, the facility was designed with with total flexibility in order not to inhibit any type of learning and instruction. This flexibility includes:

> Infinite access floors and ceilings to permit the use of multimedia materials wherever required.
> Fully adjustable overhead lighting to permit selection of light levels appropriate to the various medias being used (front projection, rear projection, television, casual reading, intensive study, etc.).
> Demountable walls to permit reorganization of walled space.
> Mobile shelving stacks to permit the 45,000 shelved print and non-print material collections to be relocated in any

floor plan as required to support the learning or instruction of the day.

Totally individual units of furniture (all single student, individual and portable carrels, tables, chairs, etc.).

A series of multi-channel wireless audio transmission loops throughout the entire facility to permit simultaneous group and individual instruction without interfering with other individuals and allowing sound motion picture projectors and televisions to be used for group listening and viewing any place on the main floor of the facility without disturbing the "traditional library atmosphere."

Individually remote student controlled color video tape players to allow each student to review and learn at his own rate.

Large modular two-place tutorial instruction booths (each with chalk surfaces, projection surfaces and work surfaces) to provide ample standing and sitting space for a variety of tutorial needs.

Total microform circulation along with cassette players— circulated in the same manner and as freely as books.

Credentialed instructors assigned to the main floor of the Learning Center during all hours of operation and

. . . all these activities within the atmosphere and services of a Traditional Library."

Schnectady Educational Opportunity Center.

(Letter to the author from Thad Raushi, Counselor Coordinator, Schenectady County Community College).

"The Schenectady Educational Opportunity Center is a State University of New York progrm operated by Schenectady County Community College. It provides skill training and academic development programs, in line with employment demands, to meet the needs of educationally and/or economically disadvantaged persons. Upgrading for job mobility, providing skills which qualify persons for college enrollment, and offering counseling services (vocational, educational, personal, referral) open to the community at large is a major thrust of the program. There is no cost to the student and enrollment is continuous, based upon class openings. Instruction is highly individualized and ongoing cooperation with community agencies and businesses assists in meeting the individual's educational and employment placement needs. The recently developed self-contained mobile classroom and separate mobile counseling van add to the Center's outreach of services to populations not able to utilize the downtown building. Program Uniqueness:

> *Continuous Enrollment and Individualized Instruction* Enrollment in classes may take place any week throughout the year as there are openings. New students begin each Monday of the week with orientation and basic academic assessment.
> While in a class a student works at a level and learning rate appropriate for that person. Instruction is, therefore, individualized and progress is based on the individual student's own rate of learning. Time limits for course instruction is set appropriately for the individual student.
> *Mobile Counseling and Instructional Units* Self-contained mobile units have been just acquired to reach population which otherwise could not take advantage of the Center. The instructional unit can accommodate 19 persons at one time is designed for handling larger instructional equipment (e.g. keypunch machines). An office area is also located within the classroom on wheels. The self-powered counseling unit accommodates 3 persons in an office atmosphere and will be utilized for outreach and counseling services.
> *Counseling Program* Counseling services, which are available to all students, is an integral part of the educational experience. Personal development and goal setting, educational and vocational exploration, referral work, are some of the major counseling functions.
> Within an informal atmosphere both instructional and counseling staff place great emphasis on assisting students in developing a positive self concept vital for ongoing success and job mobility."

College of Du Page.
(Letter to the author from Richard L. Ducote, Dean of Learning Resources).

"Some of our more "unique" applications are as follows:
(1) Complete intershelving of all media using a simple (LC) classification.
(2) Cataloging and processing of all book and non-book materials.
(3) Independent listening and viewing in the public areas of LRC.
(4) The Human Resources Exchange.
(5) Unique film programming.
(6) Valiant efforts in the area of Instructional Design.
(7) Wide-spread computer applications with on-line circulation system, with on-line author-title look-up and serials coming very shortly.
(8) Extensive exhibits of community resources.
(9) 16mm film production.
(10) Innovative organizational structure.
(11) Interesting Bibliographic services.
(12) Free film programming for community services through a grant from National Endowment for Humanities.
(13) New color television studio.
(14) Commitment to Faculty Consulting."

Santa Barbara City College.
(Letter to the author from Robert A. Carman, Director, Learning Resource Center).
"The Learning Resources Center at Santa Barbara City College is designed to provide support services to faculty members teaching in all academic areas and to all students. The LRC includes a Reading Lab, a Writing Lab, and a Math Lab, each staffed with permanent faculty, classified tutors, and student tutors. These labs are centered around basic developmental and remedial courses in English and Mathematics, but offer extensive support to other courses, to students referred by other instructors, and to walk-in students. A most important part of the LRC is the Tutorial Center which trains, supervises, and manages a corps of tutors who work in the other parts of the learning center. The physical facilities of the LRC will be greatly expanded in the coming year with the completion of a new building designed to house individualized instruction activities such as Audio-Tutorial courses, multimedia learning packages, etc. The

work of the Learning Resources Center is complemented by an Instructional Materials Center also due for expansion into new facilities in 1974-75. The IMC includes Audio-Visual Services and media production facilities.

"Our tutorial program is outstanding. It has been in operation since 1970 and now employs roughly forty to fifty tutors plus volunteer and for-credit tutors. The tutors are trained, supervised, and evaluated, and used very effectively in remedial reading, writing, and remedial math instruction, and in every academic area of the college.

"Our Math Lab program is unique and has received much attention from schools across the country. We enroll about 1,300 students each year in a remedial arithmetic course taught on an individualized basis using Programmed Instruction and tutors. Studies have shown that the program is more effective than conventional instructional strategies and costs a great deal less. Special programmed instructional materials have been developed for the course.

"We find that tutors, used in a carefully planned, structured way, with carefully prepared instructional materials, are the key to our success with low ability students."

Cuyahoga Community College.

(Letter to the author from Richard C. Decker, Director, Educational Media Center).

"Faculty and professional staff have available any and all media production services and facilities to design, develop, and produce any type of media required—simple or elaborate art; slides or photographs; tapes, both stereo and mono; simple or complex television productions; and silent or sound motion pictures, both 8mm and 16mm. All of these services are available to faculty and other professional staff but students do not have direct access to such. This is due to our level of sophistication and workload and a conscious decision on the part of the college at the time of establishing the EMC. Such services have been made available to students, minimally, through faculty requests for their students. I am currently exploring the possibilities of making available, such services through some area within the college. In my travels throughout the country, I was able to identify several institutions which have done a great deal along this line and made very fine facilities and equipment available for student use in producing materials for classroom presentations.

"The most important function in helping clientele in my opinion, is an effective design/development process. Without a recognized structure, the clientele are unable to realize the benefits of the available services and make really effective use of such."

Wing Learning Center.
(Letter to the author from Robert W. Skinner, United States Air Force, Chief, Wing Learning Center, Williams Air Force Base).

"The learning centers here at Williams AFB provide support to both the T-37 and T-38 phases of training through the audio/visual media. The two centers combined have a total of 47 student study carrels of which 5 are cockpit type, 8 for strictly study purposes, and the rest have sound on slide and/or super 8mm self-contained equipment in them. From 53 super 8mm film programs and approximately 80 sound on slide programs just about every phase of flight and just about every emergency procedure that student pilots may encounter can be studied in detail on the ground in a relaxed atmosphere. Thus we are able to help reduce the psychological and physiological stress that always accompanies the task of piloting an aircraft."

Los Medanos Community College.
(From the *Los Medanos College News*, vol 1, no. 1, Spring, 1974, p. 4).

The heart of the teaching and learning process at Los Medanos College, designed to supply the physical resources and pump the life-giving knowledge throughout the campus, is a unique four-story tower known at the "Learning Center."

Designed as a "building within a building" it is the baby of A. Don Donatelli, LMC Director of Learning Resources who is responsible for working with faculty and other college staff in the development of new approaches to teaching and learning.

He describes the Learning Center, physically, as being "the center of the college campus."

"But more important," Donatelli says, "the Learning Center is functionally in the center of the college's instructional program."

The resources themselves range from the traditional, hard-bound research books to electronic slide-and-sound systems for individual study and extend beyond to a categorized list of people in the local business-manufacturing community whose expertise can be tapped.

Here is how Donatelli describes the services provided throughout the four floors of the Learning Center:

The first floor contains 86 independent student study carrels, each equipped with appropriate audio visual study equipment. In addition to the study carrels, there are two soundproof small group study carrels, there are two soundproof small group study rooms equipped for group study of audio-visual multi-media materials. Audio-visual materials available will range from slides, filmstrips, models, study prints, audio recordings, slide-cassette kits, 8mm and 16mm motion picture films and video taped materials.

The second floor contains the office of the director, a planning area, campus audio-visual services, recording rooms, study carrels, an educational computer terminal and a media production center.

The third floor serves the students and faculty with the more traditional library services such as reference services, circulation of books and other printed materials, microfilm study (both viewing and printing) and periodicals (magazines and newspapers) to fill out a broad reference collection. The third floor also contains study rooms, as well as an instructional computer terminal.

The fourth floor provides for the storage and shelving of the general book collection as well as a professional collection for the faculty. Ample carrel study spaces are provided for browsing through materials.

110

Printed materials to be handed out in classes will be produced for faculty through the central secretarial pool and duplication center which are a part of learning resources at Los Medanos College.

The Learning Center at Los Medanos is one of the most comprehensive, current and well-planned facilities in the country and will be on the list of places for educators to visit along with the rest of the college's fine facilities.

Evaluating the Learning Center

The author's research on learning centers in the community college indicated that only 56.7 percent of centers were regularly evaluated. Of these, 34 percent sent questionnaires to faculty, 32 percent sent questionnaires to students, 28 percent interviewed faculty, 18 percent interviewed students, and 14 percent ran cost benefit analyses. Four percent used all of the above techniques.

Evaluation of a learning center presents special problems. Unlike a course, there is no set of competencies that each user of the center will want to possess. Each student, each instructor approaches with a different set of objectives—some fairly clearly defined, some muddled. What then can be examined? Can it ever be determined if learning is "better" because of the center?

Traditionally evaluation can be easily made through a cumulative inventory of equipment, distribution of book collection and nonprint collection by subject areas, square feet, shelf space, seating space, etc. Also, students and faculty can be surveyed or interviewed to learn their level of satisfaction with the learning center.

However, assessing the effectiveness of nontraditional components such as a tutorial center may call for new methodologies. For example, if students are enrolled on a credit/no credit basis, it is difficult to measure the effectiveness of such a service. All tutors and supervisors should cooperate closely with faculty so that they can work together on student weaknesses and note

111

progress accurately. Also, a simple but foolproof system of logging students in and out must be developed in order to keep track of cumulative hours of tutoring each student receives. An obvious longitudinal measure to be made is that of student success in classes in which he is tutored.

Evaluating the output of a career guidance center is also complex due to the diverse objectives of users. Basic to the evaluation of a career center is determining its basic goal: is the center to provide job information only or is it further to supply people with a methodology for exploring and choosing a career?

Determining the usefulness of the instructional development component will probably begin with the needs assessment discussed above. But evaluation here must be an ongoing process. A careful record of the most frequent and infrequent users of this service should be noted. Instructors in each group can then be asked appropriate questions concerning instructional development.

Perhaps what is most needed are some comparative studies which examine the operation of a traditionally organized library as compared with that of a learning center. Such studies raise large methodological issues. Without such work, however, there can be little chance of success in assessing the impact of learning centers, for while the centers offer more services and services in somewhat different ways, the impact of more traditional services in new environments is difficult to assess. Certainly, however, the LC is more efficient in use of resources and is a totally more exciting and up-to-date institution than was the old one!

Appendixes

Appendix A

Survey on Instructional Techniques

DeANZA COLLEGE LEARNING CENTER

To: All faculty
From: Bill Keehn, Chet Platt
Re: De Anza College faculty interviews

In the next several weeks the Instructional Research Office will be conducting a series of faculty interviews. The purpose of these interviews is to identify the instructional techniques instructors have found to be effective with various subjects, to obtain their views on other instructional techniques, and to collect suggestions on how instruction can be further improved. Information from the interviews will be collated and analysed as an aid to developing feasible actions which will effectively help the De Anza faculty to improve instruction.

Responses to specific survey questions will be sought to provide a basic, common structure to the information collected. Comments which go beyond the questions are very much desired, however, and will be used to ensure that the questions do not give an unintentionally limited view of the teaching/learning process.

A representative sample of the faculty will be used for these interviews. Each interviewee will review a copy of the whole questionnaire, get any necessary clarifications from the interviewer, respond to the questions in sequence, and make additional comments. The interviewer will record the instructor's views on another copy of the questionnaire.

Responses are intended to be related to one course. Instructors teaching several courses in significantly different ways may be asked to participate in completing more than one questionnaire.

Confidentiality of individual responses will be fully maintained.

We look forward to speaking with many of you in the not too distant future.

You continuing support is very much appreciated.

Survey on Instructional Techniques

Instructor _____

Course _____

The purpose of this interview is to identify the instructional techniques instructors have found to be effective with various subjects, to obtain their views on other instructional techniques, and to collect suggestions on how instruction can be further improved. Information from the interview will be collated and analysed as an aid to developing feasible actions which will effectively help the De Anza Faculty to improve instruction.

Responses to specific survey questions are sought to provide a basic, common structure to the information collected. Comments which go beyond the questions are very much desired, however, and will be used to ensure that the questions do not give an unintentionally limited view of the teaching/learning process.

Each interviewee will review a copy of the whole questionnaire, get any necessary clarifications from the interviewer, respond to the questions in sequence, and make additional comments. The interviewer will record the instructor's views on another copy of the questionnaire.

Responses are intended to be related to one course. Instructors teaching several courses in significantly different ways may be asked to participate in completing more than one questionnaire.

Confidentiality of individual responses will be fully maintained.

INSTRUCTIONAL TECHNIQUES

1. *It is commonly felt that the instructional technique used in community colleges more often than any other is lecturing.* Is this true for you in this course?
2. a. If so, why do you do so? (e.g. best way of accomplishing instructional intentions for the course, only feasible way in classes averaging___.)
   b. If not, what technique(s) do you use instead of, or in addition to, lecturing?
3. For this course audio-visual support (please specify the kind):
   a. Is extensively used.

117

    b. Would be used more frequently if preparation time and resources were available.

    c. Is moderately used and more is not needed.

    d. Is inappropriate

4. Forgetting practical constraints for a moment, what instructional techniques do you believe should ideally be used to enable students who enroll in the course to learn from it what you feel they should learn?

INSTRUCTIONAL INTENTIONS

5. a. If you give students a written statement of what they are expected to gain from this course, may a copy be obtained for use in compiling data on such statements?

    b. If you do not, what are your reasons for this?

    c. If you do not, (or if the written statement of your intentions needs amplification) can you classify what you intend to have your students learn in terms of the categories on the attachment (adopted from a set developed by a committee of college and university examiners)?

    d. If your instructional intentions are compatible with the attached classifications, please describe them in terms you feel are suitable.

6. Would you say that your intentions in this course

    a. Are what you believe students realistically require,—for a 2-year career program, a 4-year career (transfer) program, or general enhancement of competencies for living?

    b. Have been scaled down because of practical constraints (e.g. too wide a spread in the beginning competencies of students, large classes, inadequate student motivation) from the competencies students actually will need for careers or living?

MOTIVATION

7. In your opinion, what are the reasons students need to have the competencies you intend them to gain from this course?

8. What requirements are students satisfying when they take this course (e.g. a 2-year career program, a 4-year career (transfer) program, general education.)

9. If this course were not required in any sense, what percent of the students who now enroll do you estimate would still enroll?

10. Please estimate the ratio between (1) the instructional time you devote in this course to motivating students (convincing them of

the subject's interest or value to them) and (2) the time you devote to helping them to acquire information, skills, or attitudinal change (other than acceptance of the course).

EVALUATION OF LEARNING

11. For certain kinds of learning and/or for certain people, it appears to be essential for learners to have sufficient opportunities (in addition to tests) to try out the competencies they are expected to achieve and to get information about results and corrections quickly. In this course:
    a. Such feedback is provided.
    b. Would be desirable but is not feasible.
    c. Is not appropriate.
12. Please identify what you use to evaluate a students' learning in this course instead of, or in addition to, the feedback method.
    a. Student performance on tests, primarily identification, recall, or production of definite answers (True-False, multiple choice free, short answers, routine mathematical process, e.g., quadratic equations).
    b. Student performance on paper and pencil tests demonstrating ability to devise and carry out a sequence of cognitive actions, analyse, synthesize, etc.
    c. Student performance on non-paper-and-pencil demonstrations.
    d. Your subjective estimate—without support from test results.
    e. Student estimates.
    f. Other.
13. a. Are your students informed at the beginning of the course (by your written statement of intentions or oral descriptions) what specific performance will be required of them in your tests?
    b. If you do not relate your tests closely to your statement of instructional intentions, why is this?
14. As a result of your assessment of the level of student learning in this course, do you feel that:
    a. No significant changes in instructional design (intentions, techniques, evaluation) are needed (everything can, of course, be improved).
    b. Significant changes are currently being planned or carried out.
    c. Significant changes are desirable but require a major effort not presently feasible. (Please comment)

SUGGESTIONS FOR IMPROVEMENT

15. What actions by De Anza or the district, legislative changes, or other things can you suggest which will help instructors to improve their instructional skill?

Appendix B

Survey of Learning Center Facilities Requirements

Name of function (See list, "LC Functions and Related Functions Housed in the LC") _____
Date of Survey _____
Administrator immediately responsible for function _____
To whom does he/she report _____
Person interviewed to obtain the following information _____
1. Present Operations (Significant planned changes will be covered below)

   A. Major, continuing processes or activities performed?

   B. Results expected (description, not estimation of quantity or quality)?

   C. Who utilizes/receives/benefits from the results, (e.g. students, faculty, community members, etc.)?

   D. What conditions can cause significant obstacles to performing this function?

   E. During what hours are the activities performed?

   F. On what days of the week?

G. During what months?

H. If these hours/days/months are sometimes changed because of budget deficiencies, please describe.

II. Relationships with other functions.
   A. From which function(s) does this one receive "input" (i.e. clients, information, processed work)?

   B. To which function(s) does this one send clients, information processed work, etc.?

   C. What conditions in receiving "input" or supplying "output" to other functions can cause significant obstacles to effective, efficient operations.

III. Persons required to staff this function:

   A. Administrators

   B. Faculty members

   C. Classified staff

   D. Paraprofessional aides

   E. Student assistants: man-hours/day

IV. Space Requirements
   A. Staff
      1. Professional/administrative
      2. Technical support
      3. Clerical support
      4. Student workers
      5. Other work space
   B. Equipment
      Item   *Area*

C. "Clients" (students, faculty, etc.)
   1. Average number using facility
   2. Peak number using facility

   3. Client work or student space: Area/Person_____
      Total Area_____

Significant   Minor
Full-time Part-Time Part-Time

No. Area/Person   Total Area

   D. Storage Spaces
      Kind   *Area*

IV. Other Significant Facilities Requirements
   A. Particular location on campus (Specify)

   B. Particular location in building e.g. access from outside. (Specify)

   C. Traffic flow inside building (Specify)

   D. Access/utilization requirements for handicapped

   E. Sound control

   F. Lighting

   G. Electric Wiring and Outlets

   H. Telephones

   I. Security

   J. Others (Specify):

Assessment of Needs of this Function
1. Current operation
   _____ Satisfactory
   _____ Minor improvements needed
   _____ Significant improvements are needed and planning is under way (See below)
   _____ Significant improvements are needed
II. If improvements are needed but plans are not yet under way, briefly describe the needs under the appropriate categories.
   A. Amount of space

   B. Arrangement of space

   C. Other facilities requirements

   D. Staffing

   E. Relationships with other functions

   F. Other

Planned Changes—Short-range
1. If changes in the operation of this function which are likely to be made within 12 months are under active consideration, please estimate the expected consequences by recording relevant information below, keyed to item number from the above survey form.

Planned changes—Long-range
1. Please do the same for any which are likely to be made beyond 12 months from now.

LC FUNCTIONS AND RELATED FUNCTIONS HOUSED IN THE LC

I. *Learning-Center Functions*
A. Technical Services
    1. Research for acquisitions
       a. Books
       b. Periodicals and pamphlets
       c. Non-print media
    2. Ordering, receiving, accounting
       a. Books and pamphlets
       b. Periodicals
       c. Non-print media
    3. Cataloging and maintenance of catalogs
       a. Print
       b. Audio material
       c. Other non-print media
    4. Shelving/storing
       a. Books
       b. Periodicals and microfilm
       c. Other media
    5. Mending/binding/laminating etc. of print media
    6. Purchase, installation, maintenance of AV equipment
    7. Production of photographic media
    8. Production of graphic media
    9. Production of audio media
   10. Reprographic services
B. Public Services
    1. General and reserve book collection: Control of circulation, maintenance of records.
    2. Special collections: control maintenance of records, etc.
       a. Legal material
       b. Archive material
       c. Other professional material
       d. Maps
       e. Microfiche
    3. Periodicals: maintenance and control of hard copy and microfilm collections, circulation, and supervision of microfiche reader
    4. Reference materials: maintenance and control of collection and provision of information

5. Listening room
6. Circulation of AV equipment and media
7. Institutional research/grant application services
8. Instructional development services
    a. Assistance to faculty members for improvement/development of courses/curricula
    b. Enhancement of instructional techniques (as part of faculty development)
9. Development and supervision of independent studies
10. Provision of study areas: individual students
11. Provision of conference areas: small groups
12. TV and AV media viewing facilities: large groups
13. TV and AV media viewing facilities: small groups
14. TV and AV media viewing facilities: individuals
15. Facilities for AV media production by students and faculty
16. Student typing facilities
17. Preparation and control of displays and exhibits
18. Faculty reading room

II. *Related Functions Housed in the LC*
    A. Language Laboratory
    B. Educational Diagnostic Clinic
    C. Tutorial Center
    D. Career Center
    E. Skills Center
    F. Coordinated Learning Laboratory
    G. Open (equipment/media-sharing) Laboratory (under consideration) to consolidate some services of:
        1. Educational Diagnostic Clinic
        2. Tutorial Center
        3. Independent Studies
        4. Coordinated Learning Laboratory
        5. Career Center

III. *Related Functions Not Housed in LC—For Possible Consideration*
    A. Reading Laboratory (under consideration for LC)
    B. Writing Laboratory (formation under consideration)
    C. College Readiness Program
    D. Nursing Autotutorial Skills Laboratory

E. Autotech Autotutorial program

F. Bilingual Center

G. Computer-assisted instruction

IV. *Needs Not Being Met by Any Current Function*

Please identify such needs and provide an estimate of the requirements for meeting them by use of the form "Survey of LC Facilities Requirements"

STAFFING MODEL

GOAL	OBJECTIVES/ACTIVITIES	PRESENT STAFF	ADDITIONAL STAFF REQUIREMENTS	TIMELINE FOR HIRING ADDITIONAL STAFF
1. Provide a comprehensive collection of print and non print materials.	1.1. Acquire print and non print materials for LRC and Divisions. Books Pamphlets Periodicals Newspapers Microform Films (8 & 16 mm) Filmstrips Slides Video tapes/cassettes Audio tapes/cassettes Records	(Books) _____ + Clerk + 1 Clerk (Periodicals, etc.) _____ + 1 Clerk (Non-Print) _____ + 1 Clerk	1 Library Media Technical Assistant. 1 Clerk The staff increase is essential as we increase our non print resources and expand our capabilities for their use in the LRC. The LMTA and Clerk will be utilized primarily in the ordering and processing of periodicals and non print materials. The LMTA will be particularly helpful in performing paraprofessional assignments and thus relieve the professional staff to work with faculty, acquire materials and develop a system of cataloging and processing the materials The Clerk will be helpful in reducing our reliance on part time-student	July 1, 1974 July 1, 1974
	1.2 Implement centralized system to catalog, classify and process print and non print matters for LRC and Divisions. Books Pamphlets Periodicals Newspapers Microform	_____ + 4 part-time students. _____ + 10 part-time students. None. Procedures for the cataloging, classifying and processing of non print materials have not been developed.		

Goal	Objectives / Materials	Staff	Personnel Needs	Target Date
	Films Filmstrips Videotapes/cassettes Audio tapes/cassettes Records		assistants. The turn over is high among the student assistants and considerable time is spent in training them.	
	1.3. Explore automation of operations of LRC: acquisition, circulation, retrieval and reference.	NONE	College Systems analyst to do study.	July 1, 1974
	1.4 Explore use of time share services to avail LRC of present information.	NONE		
2. Provide services and equipment for the college community to retrieve and use print and non print materials.	2.1 Assist students and staff in locating and using materials by ——. housed in the LRC. Books Pamphlets Periodicals Newspapers Microform Filmstrips Slides Films (8 & 16mm) Video tapes/cassettes Audio tapes/cassettes Records	All certificated staff coordinated Specialist) with ——/Clerk. Student workers primarily responsible for assisting students with all non print materials in LRC.	1 Certificated person (Media background and/or preparation in use of materials in all formats. This is essential as we expand our non print materials.	July 1, 1974
	2.2. Obtain materials not currently in LRC. Books Pamphlets Periodicals	Certificated staff and Clerks, Print materials are obtained through InterLibrary Loans,		

GOAL	OBJECTIVES/ACTIVITIES	PRESENT STAFF	ADDITIONAL STAFF REQUIREMENTS	TIMELINE FOR HIRING ADDITIONAL STAFF
2. (Continued) Provide services and equipment for the college community to retrieve and use print and non print materials	Newspapers Microform Filmstrips Slides Films (8 & 16mm) Video tapes/cassettes Audio tapes/cassettes	E.R.I.C., etc. Most non print materials with the exception of 16mm films must be purchased rather than rented. Currently 16mm film rentals are coordinated by _____.		
	2.2. (continued) Obtain materials not currently in LRC.	With expansion of LRC and physical proximity of staff, the same clerks could handle requests for all materials not in LRC including film rentals.		
	2.3. Maintain circulation system for materials.	_____/2 Clerks 6 students	L.M.T.A.	July 1, 1975
	Books Pamphlets Periodicals Newspapers Microform Films (8 & 16mm) Filmstrips Slides Video tapes/cassettes Audio tapes/cassettes	Cefaloni/Clerk Students Circulation of non print media for independent study in the LRC is currently supervised by _____. Circulation of non print media outside	With the expansion of the LRC, the circulation of all non print materials in the LRC and to the Divisions would be coordinated thru one office.	

2. (continued) Provide services and equipment for the college community to retrieve and use print and non print materials.

Records

2.4. Provide equipment and assistance for using non print and microfilm materials in the LRC.
16 mm projectors
8 mm projectors
8 mm loop projectors
slide projectors
overhead projectors
audio tape recorders/pl
video tape
video cassette players
video monitors

2.5 Maintain equipment circulation system to the Divisions for use of non print materials.

16 mm projectors
8 mm projectors
8 mm loop projectors
slide projectors
filmstrip projectors
overhead projectors
opaque projectors
audio tape recorders/players
audio cassette players
video tape players
video cassette players

the LRC is supervised by _____/Clerk Students.

Currently, slide projectors and audio cassette players are used most frequently. Other pieces of equipment will be added with LRC expansion.

_____ & Clerks

Clerk.

The additional certificated person and L.M.T.A. (see 2.1 & 2.2.) and Clerk would work closely in the use & circulation of non print materials and equipment.

see 2.2 & 2.3

GOAL	OBJECTIVES/ACTIVITIES	PRESENT STAFF	ADDITIONAL STAFF REQUIREMENTS	TIMELINE FOR HIRING ADDITIONAL STAFF
2. (Continued)	video monitors record players P.A. systems 2.6. Implement program of positive maintenance and repair for all audiovisual equipment. work is being done on Projectors (all kinds) Audio tape & cassette recording & playing equipment. Public address system equipment Video cameras Video tape and cassette players Video production Editing & production equipment Mounting equipment Laminating equipment Duplicating equipment Printing equipment Photocopy equipment Photography development & production Film production, editing & splicing equipment	——— +1 part-time technician. Currently much of the the full develop- an as needed basis. Much equipment through-out the college needs to be inspected and maintained.	Part-time Repair technician should become full time. This will permit the full develop-ment and implemen-tation of preventive maintenance and repair program. 1 Full time Repair Technician Required to maintain & repair new equipment used in independent study, video production, editing & production, etc. Maintenance of video equipment will be of particular importance.	July 1, 1974 July 1, 1975 Second repair technician

132

Goal	Objectives/Activities	Responsibility	Resources Needed
3. Provide informational, instructional & learning services for the college community.	Film inspection & repair of equipment		1 Clerk
	3.1 Revised (update) Student Handbook.	Certificated staff Clerk (1975-1976)	An additional typist clerk is needed to assist in carrying out the Objectives/ Activities related to the Goal. The only Clerk Typist (_____) is needed full time by the Director.
	3.2 Explore possible approaches to development of LRC Newsletter	Certificated staff Clerk (1974-1975)	
	3.3 Prepare materials in written and audio-visual format on the functions, facilities, services, materials & equipment of the LRC.	Certificated staff Technical staff Clerk (1974-75)	
	3.4 Determine faculty and administrator needs and interests regarding material and information and disseminate the same to them.	Certificated staff Clerk (1974-75)	
	3.5 Give orientation sessions on the LRC as requested by classes in various disciplines.	Clerk Student	
	3.6 Offer Course: Use of Library Resources, each semester.	Clerk Student	
	3.7 Initiate new LRC related courses.	Clerk Student	
	3.8 Offer cultural and literary programs.	Clerk Student	

GOAL	OBJECTIVES/ACTIVITIES	PRESENT STAFF	ADDITIONAL STAFF REQUIREMENTS	TIMELINE FOR HIRING ADDITIONAL STAFF
	3.9 Coordinate diagnostic learning services to students	NONE	1 certificated person. This person, the Learning Specialist, will work with students to determine their learning styles & with faculty to arrange appropriate learning activities. The learning specialist will train student tutors. This person works closely with the Development-Design Specialist in assisting faculty in the development and improvement of instructional techniques.	July 1, 1974
	3.10 Prepare students to serve as tutors/learning assistants.	NONE		
	3.11 Arrange individual and group tutorials.	NONE activities. The learning specialist will train		
	3.12 Coordinate independent learning activities for students.	NONE	See 3.9 This would be another aspect of the work of the Learning Specialist. It would involve coordination with faculty & other LRC staff.	
	3.13 Conduct educational program for Learning Center Technicians.	NONE	It is proposed that West Valley & De Anza cooperate in developing and implementing	July 1, 1975 but more likely July 1, 1976

Goal	Objective		
	3.4 Explore possibilities for coordinating Career Development services to students.	Certificated staff (1974-75) This objective would be implemented with assistance of Counseling Staff.	this program. A minimum of 1/2 time certificated person would be required. (The other 1/2 time person would be supplied by De Anza)
4. Provide instructional development and production services to members of the college community.	4.1 Give consultive assistance to faculty in various aspects of instructional development, i.e., organizing instructional services, developing learning objectives, planning learning experiences, planning or selecting media, planning evaluation devices.	Certificated staff: Development Design Development-Design Specialist	July 1, 1974 Specialist will work with faculty in all aspects of instructional development & related experimentation (4.1 & 4.2) Will participate in planning, coordinating & offering short course workshops & seminars related to instructional development, (4.3), and staff development program (5.5). Will be involved in informational, instructional and learning services of LRC (3).

GOAL	OBJECTIVES/ACTIVITIES	PRESENT STAFF	ADDITIONAL STAFF REQUIREMENTS	TIMELINE FOR HIRING ADDITIONAL STAFF
4. (Continued)	4.2 Provide opportunities for faculty to experiment with instructional approaches.	Limited		
	4.3. Offer short courses, workshops, seminars on instructional development. See 4.1. (Could also be included under Goals 3 & 5).	NONE		
	4.4 Plan and prepare instructional media, (single or multi) i.e., Photopaper prints Slide series Filmstrips Motion pictures Transparencies Displays Graphic art work Video presentations	——— Due to lack of staff ——— & equipment, the LRC Photographer (part-time)	is unable to meet the faculty requests for services. This functional area will be greatly expanded with the completion of the LRC addition. Part-time photographer should become full time. This will allow assistance to faculty for all types of photography, development of film & duplication of slides, etc. Production Technician will produce audio recordings & duplicate	July 1, 1974

136

Objective	Description	Staffing	Date
	tapes, assist with video production, assemble A-V presentations, develop and maintain schedules for production of audio-visual materials. Television Specialist will be required to coordinate production, editing, distribution of all programs in & out of new studio.		July 1, 1975
	Graphic Artist will be required for production of artwork for A-V materials and video presentations. These staff members together with present staff will be available to assist faculty and students who wish to prepare instructional media. (4.5)		July 1, 1976
4.5 Provide opportunities for faculty & students to prepare instructional media.		———— (Limited basis)	
4.6 Produce typed originals & prepare printed copy of instructional materials.	Preparation (typing) & printed materials production is a basic support to faculty. Materials they develop for instructional	1 Clerk typist 2 machine operators	July 1, 1975

137

STAFFING (continued)

GOAL	OBJECTIVES/ACTIVITIES	PRESENT STAFF	ADDITIONAL STAFF REQUIREMENTS	TIMELINE FOR HIRING ADDITIONAL STAFF
4. Continued	Print Photocopy Ditto mimeograph		purposes must be typed and duplicated. 1 Clerk typist	July 1, 1975
5. Participate in institutional planning & educational development of the college district.	5.1 Participate in planning & implementing on going activities of the college, i.e., serve on standing & special committees.	Director will be involved in most development and planning Objectives and activities. Certificated staff		
	5.2. Participate in planning & implementing instructional programs. Work with divisions related to current and future educational program planning & selecting learning materials & equipment.	Certificated staff	The staff requested in relationship to other goals will be important in liaison work with Divisions.	
	5.3 Plan space, equipment, materials requirements of LRC.	Certificated staff		
	5.4. Participate in planning for Mission Campus.	Certificated staff	RELEASE TIME	

5. (Continued)	5.5 Participate in planning & implementing staff development program (see also Goals 3 & 4)	Certificated staff	Additional staff hired, particularly Development-Design Specialist & Learning Specialist will be extremely helpful in planning & implementing staff development program.	
6. Engage in cooperative interaction with community & county agencies & groups & educational institutions.	6.1. Utilize services & resources of and give support to county agencies, i.e., educational media center, Cooperative Information Network.	Director will be involved in most development and planning of Objectives and Activities. Certificated staff Certificated staff		
	6.2. Explore & participate in cooperative projects with community colleges & other educational institutions.			
	6.3. Explore areas for cooperation with De Anza College, i.e., Staff Development, Learning Center Technicians Program.	Certificated staff	Approximately the equivalent of one half time certificated person will be required for Learning Center Technicians Program.	July 1, 1975 more likely July 1, 1976.

139

Example Management Statements

A. Instructional Development Specialist
Objectives

1. Work as leader of the ID team, trying to work during the year with at least one instructor from each division.
2. Develop a learning package for each of the slide programs on equipment usage. 16mm, overhead, tape recorder, Wrico sign maker, etc. Each package will include:
   a. Course activities sheet
   b. Introduction and objectives of unit
   c. Evaluation sheet
   d. Information sheet
   e. Worksheet
3. Complete designing, equipping and facilitation of ID and coordinated Learning Lab.
4. Produce the Spring issue of *Noticias* on cassettes.
5. Complete and instigate the staff development plan for LC to be operating by October 31, 1973.
6. Serve on the Steering Committee of the Tutorial Center.
7. Supervise the "Alternative Learning Environment and Strategy" project.
8. Complete a set of written procedures for all AV and ID activities.

9. Develop and instigate a plan for instructional development and media production (with evening technician) for evening faculty.

10. Develop a long range written plan for the printing operation at De Anza.

11. Plan an audio visual seminar to be held yearly for media professionals and for personnel from industry and business.

12. Develop an internship and grant relationship between De Anza, San Jose State's Department of Instructional Technology, College of San Mateo, and the Veteran's Hospital.

B. **Administrative Specialist**

Objectives

Personal/Professional

To complete an administrative internship in preparation for one day assuming a vertically higher position, probably either a Dean of Instruction, an academic vice presidency, the Dean of a graduate media program, or the directorship of a large university library. Administrative tasks to be enumerated and assigned primarily by the Dean of Instruction and some by the President. This open-ended objective must include specific tasks in the areas of faculty selection, faculty evaluation, budgeteering, administrative representation off campus, etc.

Administrative/Professional

1. With the other administrators in the Instruction Office, plan a faculty/staff development program which by June 30, 1974, will have a written plan and a slide/tape format for presentation to ours and other faculties and at professional meetings. The program should have been actualized in a number of areas, including the presentation (with the two other members of the team) of an instructional development workshop, on site visitations to selected classrooms (by instructor request) with subsequent team prescription activity for experimental educational variation for the classes, short term exchanges of staff members with neighboring schools, etc.

2. To develop by September, 1974, a monograph on the state-of-the-art for learning centers. This monograph will be the result of a CAEMAT-supported study of community col-

lege learning centers and a few selected four year colleges and universities throughout the U.S.

3. To present the second annual symposium on learning environments. This symposium to be on learning centers and to be jointly sponsored by CJCA, DAC, the Learning Resource Association of California Community Colleges, and the California Community College Media Association. To initiate this nationwide symposium.

    a. during the summer of 1973, dates, a general program, and facility scheduling will be completed;

    b. during the fall quarter, complete planning and advertising for the symposium.

The symposium should take place during the winter quarter and will be evaluated by a group from the sponsoring organizations and local colleges.

4. To direct research office activity so that by the end of the school year, the office will have its goals clearly stated in writing, the faculty will be aware of the office's services, and two year plan for its continuance will have been written.

5. To work with the diagnostic learning personnel to integrate their program into the continuum of college educational services and to make this program visible and conceptually understandable to the personnel themselves, the total college community, and educators from other institutions.

6. In concert with all Learning Center personnel, and the Instruction Office, plan for the most effective space utilization of the building. Have a plan in writing by June 30, 1974.

7. In order to reacquaint myself with some of the newest thinking in the more traditional areas of learning centers, attend the CLA statewide and the ALA national meetings. Probably speak at CLA on learning centers.

8. Serve as a member of the ID team.

Innovative

To produce the following:

    a. A slide/tape package on the Cooperative Information Network. To be completed by August 21, 1973.

    b. A slide/tape package on the concept of the Learning Center. To be completed by October 30, 1973.

c. A slide/tape program on the DAC instructional development system. To be completed by October 1, 1973.
d. A printed booklet on the missions of De Anza College.
To be completed by September 15, 1973.

Index

145